Donated by
Joseph and Diane Bast
to The Heartland Institute
2015

MIR PUBLISHERS

ГЛЕБ АНФИЛОВ

# ФИЗИКА И МУЗЫКА

ИЗДАТЕЛЬСТВО
«ДЕТСКАЯ ЛИТЕРАТУРА»

GLEB ANFILOV

# PHYSICS and MUSIC

*Translated from the Russian
by* BORIS KUZNETSOV

MIR PUBLISHERS • MOSCOW 1966

Printed in the Soviet Union

UDC 78 + 534 (0.23) = 20

*На английском языке*

# Contents

*Chapter One.*
THE ORCHESTRA IN THE MAKING　　7

*Chapter Two.*
HOW SOUND IS PRODUCED　　55

*Chapter Three.*
RIVALS OF STRADIVARIUS　　76

*Chapter Four.*
VOICE ANALYSIS　　98

*Chapter Five.*
TONES CREATED BY THE EAR　　111

*Chapter Six.*
THE HISTORY OF TUNING　　124

*Chapter Seven.*
MUSIC FROM ELECTRICITY                         138

*Chapter Eight.*
THE WONDERS OF SOUND RECORDING                 167

*Chapter Nine.*
DR. SHOLPO'S DREAM                             187

*Chapter Ten.*
THE COMPOSER AS A PAINTER                      205

*Chapter Eleven.*
MUSIC FROM THE COMPUTER                        225

*Chapter Twelve.*
PHYSICS AND MUSIC                              240

*Index.*                                       249

CHAPTER ONE

*

# The Orchestra in the Making

Today's music lover is fortunate; he can have music whenever he wants it. He just turns on his radio, or goes to the opera-house or concert-hall, or learns to play himself. Any child with an ear for music or simply with ambitious parents may enter a music school. Yet about a hundred years ago the symphony orchestra was to be heard on festive occasions only. Three hundred years ago people had not heard of the grand piano. Four hundred years ago nobody knew what we today call the violin.

But there was music all the same—five hundred, a thousand, or ten thousand years ago. Our planet has always been both a musical workshop and a concert room. In any out-of-the-way place man has always sung, played or made things that whistle, hum or rattle. This has always been as vital to him as air: music has helped him to work, has added to his joy and taken the edge off his sorrow. Music has drawn people together, and made them feel and act as one,

In an African village of grass huts lost in the jungle a successful *safari* is usually crowned by a procession. Songs sound like triumphant battle cries. Cane flutes and pipes sing buoyantly and shrill sounds come from whistles made out of hollow coco-nuts with holes for fingers. The bamboo strings on bows twang and psalteries hollowed from whole chunks of wood hum away. Drums, the oldest of all the musical instruments, give a sharp and insistent beat. The village chief solemnly nods his head, which is topped with what looks like a baby's rattle,— a distinction for chiefs only.

In Borneo, during a wedding ceremony in a fishing village, a song floats softly over the sea and gongs ring out leisurely and rhythmically in time to the lapping of the waves. Then someone moves his hand, and everything changes. Tambourines, with seashells and dried fish heads, give out a spirited buzz. A graceful girl breaks into a provocative dance. The chains and bracelets of bells on her arms and legs jingle loudly.

In old Moscow at Shrovetide the whole of the city would indulge in merrymaking. Spring was welcomed boisterously with *gouslis* (psalteries), *goudoks* (fiddles) and *doudkas* (reed-flutes).

In China villagers used to march out into the fields for the first planting of rice to the sounds of bells, cymbals, the ancient *p'i p'a* (the lute) and the *hu ch'in* (the fiddle).

Music is everywhere. No one can do without it. Ancient religious beliefs maintained that music was not only a pleasure but a cause of many events. It could bring down droughts to harm the crops and rains to give them life. Music came from the gods, they said.

Imagine yourself in a temple in a cave dimly lit with oil lamps. People come in silently and lie with their faces to the ground. A priest appears, puts two yellow pipes to his neck and begins to pray, and the people start. No, that is not a human voice. The tune is an ominous and unnatural wheeze, wavering and gurgling, echoing from the resounding arches, and plunging the hearts in sorrow.

The pipes are called *niastaranghas*. Their sound comes from the cobweb-like device ingeniously hidden in the broad mouthpiece or, rather, neckpiece, because instead of being placed before the lips it is held to the neck. When the priest sings, the device vibrates, producing a jarring sound. Although this is hardly music the sound is frightening—exactly what was sought in ancient India to keep the credulous flock tame.

In Australia also, on the other side of the globe, there is public worship. A file of aboriginal worshippers is headed by a medicine man who carries the sacred *churinga* (whizzer) in his hand. The medicine man yells out his incantations and swings his *churinga*, filling the neighbourhood with shrill howls, hisses and whistles. The people fearfully bend their backs and drop their eyes. The *churinga* is the god's voice. The *churinga* is taboo. You must not look at it, or you will die.

Taboo, indeed! When a local materialist dared to look into the *churinga* there turned out to be no secret at all. Simply a clay jar on a sling attached to a long stick. As it is swung around, the air does the trick.

Throughout his history man has been making musical instruments of every description, varying among different peoples in different periods.

Take the bagpipe, which is so popular in some countries. It is a set of reed pipes through which air is forced by pressure on a wind-bag held under the arm. There was the trummscheidt or the trumpet marine, which was no trumpet at all. It looked like an oversized cello, with a drumming support for the strings. For some reason it was used by both men-of-war of the sail era and convents. Then there is the ubiquitous jaws' (some call it "jew's") harp, an elastic metal plate fixed at one end in a frame, while the other is free. The player grasps the frame in his jaws so that the plate, plucked with a finger, vibrates between the teeth. At one time the Aeolian harp was in vogue—a rectangular box with strings plucked by the wind and not by a musician's fingers. Then there was the serpent, a bass wind instrument with several bands shaped like a huge wriggling snake and finger-holes so large that it had to be played with gloves on.

Man has tried everything to make musical sounds. This trial and rejection has been going on for thousands of years, resulting in better and better instruments. Folk instruments have now changed beyond recognition; they have become functional, with a rich and strong sound. Yet all the smart pieces of the symphony orchestra can be traced back to them. If the reader lives in Leningrad or plans to go there, he can go through all the stages of this phenomenal process with his own eyes and ears by visiting the fabulous exhibition of musical instruments at the Institute of the Theatre and Music.

**THE SIMPLEST THING**

What is the simplest piece in a symphony orchestra? Probably, the conductor's baton. Then comes the flute. This once modest tube with finger-holes has become inseparable from musical art. Its gentle voice is both simple and pleasing.

True, the flute of today is a dainty thing with its exquisitely glistening keys and levers. No other instrument is made in gold or even platinum, but the flute sometimes is. A gold flute, however, is a rarity. For everyday use any material is good enough: wood, clay, ivory, or metal. It sounds best, as many years' experience has shown, when made of an alloy of copper and nickel, or manganese, tin and zinc.

The first flute was probably made from a cane.

Thousands of years ago an enterprising caveman broke a cane with his big hairy hands and blew over it. A sound came. His low-browed face lit up with a smile. This was a real breakthrough for the awakening mind in its discovery of things and events. Today's children are probably just as happy when they find out that they can whistle on door keys.

Just how much time passed before the next step was taken and finger-holes were made in the flute is anyone's guess. The chances are that the holes were first pierced by a boring beetle. Cave-man noticed that holed instruments sounded better and from then on pierced them himself, without waiting for a beetle to do the job. Now he could blow his flute and stop the holes with his fingers—the tone was as good as the chirping of cicadas in the woods at night.

Later on the flute came by the 'fipple', a device like the one in a policeman's whistle. Whoever made it was a true inventor, for it must have taken a good deal of thought. The fipple came to stay with the flute for thousands of years.

Made up of a fipple, a six-holed tube and a small flared head, the ancient end-blown flute moved from country to country in the ancient Orient, entertaining people at bazaars and wedding ceremonies. Then on camels' backs and on brightly painted Phoenician ships it moved to Egypt, Greece and Rome. On its way it changed its name, length and shape many times.

Finally the fipple flute came to be called the 'recorder' in England (from the obsolete 'record' for 'warble', a bird), the *flauto dolce* in Italy, and the *flute douce* in France.

After 1700 the recorder languished and was dropped from the symphony orchestra. Today it is recalled only when one wants to make the orchestra sound ancient. Its younger rival, the side-blown, transverse or German flute has lived to earn renown.

## END-BLOWN OR SIDE-BLOWN

There is, in Kiev, a remarkable ancient monument—St. Sophia's Cathedral. Architecture is not the only outstanding thing about it. The walls above the tower stairway leading to the gallery where the grand princes of Kiev Rus once walked are decorated with medallion frescoes with scenes from everyday life, painted some 900 years ago. By looking at the pictures the anointed sovereign could learn a thing or two about his subjects without having to rub elbows with them. Among these frescoes historians have found one of the world's earliest pictures of the side-blown flute.

The flutist in the picture holds his flute not lengthwise like a rifle, but crosswise as if it were an ear of maize from which he is picking the grains. The flute has no fipple and the upper end is stopped. The flutist blows across a slot with a sharp edge cut in the side of the tube, next to the end. How did these changes take place?

Probably a strolling flutist had inadvertently broken the fipple in his flute before an important performance. There was not enough time to make a new one, and the musician stopped the upper end and blew over the hole sideways. The flute remade so hastily gave out a stronger and more attractive tone. The performer was a success and won a generous fee. He passed down to his children and grandchildren the secret of how to play the flute the new way.

Whether or not this happened exactly as described we can only guess. But the fact is that the simpler side-blown flute came along after the more complicated recorder.

In the meantime the search for improvements went on. What holes should be made in the flute, large or small? Round or oval? An acoustics engineer of today would solve the problem within ten minutes. However, it baffled the ancient flutists who were innocent of physics.

The greatest trouble came from the location of the holes. It was noted at once that the pitch was lower for the finger-holes farther away from the mouth-hole or embouchure as it is called. The flute was made longer and longer to extend the tone range. But the long flute was difficult to play; the player's fingers could not reach the farthest holes. The audience, however, would not be placated: "As you're a flute-player, you should be able to play any tune!" What was the way out?

Someone hit upon the idea of drilling oblique "tunnels" instead of straight "wells" in the flute body. Then the outside holes of the "tunnels" were nearer than the inside holes. Somehow or other, the fingers could reach them. Unfortunately, the oblique holes spoiled the sound.

It was not until the latter half of the 17th century that it dawned upon flute-makers to fit keys and levers to the finger-holes. The idea was very simple: the keys stopping the farthest holes could have longer levers so that the player would not have to wring his hand.

As the story goes, Jean Baptiste Lully, the French composer of Italian origin, was the first to score for the keyed side-blown flute in his ballet *Le triomphe de l'amour* (1672). But it had only one key and oblique holes. Its voice was drowned in the orchestra and could hardly be heard.

The perfect flute, as we know it today, came into being in about the mid-19th century when Theobald Boehm, a great flute virtuoso in the Bavarian Court Orchestra, ventured to re-style his instrument. He made broad, straight holes, fitted a multitude of keys, and arranged a complex system of levers. And how smart the flute became! Since then it has been an indispensable member of the symphony orchestra as the owner of soprano, or the highest voice.

**THE SINGING REED**

This might have happened over 5,000 years ago, when the flute was still young and end-blown.

Somewhere in Africa or Asia a nomadic shepherd was peacefully sitting in his hut, playing his freshly-made pipe, when a little smudgy creature rushed in, making shrill high-pitched sounds. The nomad started, looked up and saw his little daughter with a mischievous look in her eyes and a piece of reed, cut lengthways, in her mouth. This was a 'streaker', such as country lads still delight to make from acacia pods in the spring. The girl was caught and punished. Then the strict father carefully examined his daughter's reed, turning it this way and that. A happy idea struck him to fit the reed to his pipe. He did so, working deftly with his bone knife, and played on the new contrivance. The tone had changed for the better and was easier to blow. That same evening our nomad summoned his prehistoric sheep with the weak and crackling voice of the first ancestor of today's clarinet, oboe and bassoon.

It took the primitive reed pipe several thousand years to grow into the Asiatic *zourna,* the medieval bawling shawm called *bombarde* in French and *pommern* in German, and finally the plaintive oboe which has survived to this day.

The oboe is a wooden tube with a bell at the end and two wedge-shaped pieces of reed or cane fixed face to face (called the double reed) as part of the mouthpiece. Like the flute, the oboe is studded with keys and levers. But its tone is somewhat lower, melancholic and not so ringing, which is pleasing in its own way.

The double reed is used in some other instruments. Among them is the bassoon, grumbling in an old man's baritone. In his *Wit Works Woe,* Griboyedov calls the bassoon "a wheezer" and "a strangled one". That is probably too strongly put. The bassoon has a compressed, narrow and slightly hoarse tone which makes it an excellent complement to the other tones of the orchestra.

The body of the bassoon is so long that it has to be bent back on itself and fixed. Incidentally, the Italian name for the bassoon is *fagotto,* or a bundle of sticks bound together. The stentorian and deep-toned contra or double bassoon has a still longer body. It has to be trebled back on itself. Otherwise it would be as long as a shaft and pretty difficult to carry about.

The woodwind family of instruments also includes the clarinet. It, too, is a descendant of the primitive reed pipe, though a relatively young one. It was introduced as late as 1690 by Johann Christian Denner of Nurenberg who had been led to his invention by folk shawms known by their French name *chalumeaux*.

In fact the name 'clarinet' was not mentioned before 1732.

Unlike the oboe or the bassoon, the clarinet has a straight body like a water pipe. Its main distinction, however, is in the reed. Instead of two wedge-shaped pieces, it has only one (hence the name 'single reed'). The reed is built into the mouthpiece which resembles a bird's beak. In the mouthpiece the edges of the reed overlap the slot leading into the resonating pipe. As the clarinetist blows, the reed vibrates and produces a sound—clear, slightly husky, and mellow. It blends exquisitely with the range of tone colours of the orchestra.

All these and some of the other instruments are traditionally called the woodwinds, although the material they are made of is not necessarily wood nowadays. Take, for example, the saxophone, the favourite of jazzmen. It has a conical tube of brass, an intricate system of keys, and a reed like the clarinet's.

The saxophone is the youngest of the woodwind family. It was invented by the Belgian instrument-maker Adolphe (Antoine) Sax in about 1840-41 and patented in France in 1846. Now laughing, now throbbing and now cooing, this instrument of exceptional potentialities has of late been identified mostly with jazz, light and dance music. However, it can also be serious. Incidentally, Berlioz, that refined and penetrating composer, saw a bright future for the saxophone. Some modern composers believe it can be a successful rival to the cello.

#### MUSIC AS DRUDGERY

The aurochs, the now extinct ancestor of our cattle, has descendants on the musical side also. Way back, its long pointed horns were cut off for the first time to be trimmed, cleaned and made into musical instruments whose sound, according to old ballads, "shook mountains and felled forests".

The aurochs horn was a lip-reed instrument because the player's lips pressed to its mouthpiece formed a sort of double reed.

Its thunderous voice cheered the hounds in the chase, summoned people for festivities, church service or executions, and guided warriors in battles.

Unfortunately, a big hunting horn was not at all easy to make. One had to wait until the horns on an aurochs' head had grown long enough. Nor was the aurochs in a particular hurry to grow them for musical or warlike purposes. This did not suit impatient warrior lords. For this and other reasons, the aurochs horn gave way to those made from wood and metal.

In case you have not heard about the Guzul trembita, it is a long wooden tube. Although easier to make, it still takes quite a lot of effort. In contrast to this, there is not much difficulty in making horns from brass or copper sheets. A sheet is folded into what looks like a paper cornet for groceries, the joint soldered, any rough spots smoothed down, and a horn is ready. It may be of any size, however fantastic, and far beyond what any aurochs could grow. The shape can also be chosen. The sound is clear and loud.

True, the hunting horn could not play a melody. It could only produce a single note, like a factory hooter or a car horn. The bigger the horn, the lower its tone. Yet, though crude, the horn did find its way into musical art.

In the 18th century it was popular with the Russian nobles to have hunting-horn bands. The fashion was started by one of Empress Elizabeth's court bandmasters, and everyone was at pains to copy it. They were strange bands. Can you imagine a conductor who insisted on squeezing eighty-eight pianists at one grand-piano, one for each key? Absurd, isn't it? The crazy conductor would immediately be put away in a madhouse. Yet, the hunting-horn bands were very much like this. There was a separate horn for each note (or perhaps several for loudness), and each horn was blown by a separate player. Some bands had hundreds of horns, ranging from huge pieces on supports to tiny ones the size of a palm. The band that used to play at Prince Potemkin's balls was three hundred strong!

There is no denying, it was a fine thing to dance to the loud music. But the players' lot was simply wretched. There was neither a tune to follow nor chords to construct. Like unanimated machines, they would blow their particular note and wait until it was time to come in again. There was not a moment when they could relax, and the tension of the continuous waiting was overbearing. People did the job only under the lash. This was why horn bands consisted only of serfs. Nowadays, no one would put up with drudgery like that.

### DESCENDANTS OF THE HUNTING HORN

However, the horn was not doomed to a single tone. Holes could be made in it, to be stopped by fingers, as on the flute. The shepherd's horn was made that way, for example. True, big signal horns could not have holes made in them. Metal trumpets with holes in them would sound dull and muffled. However, the performers learned one more trick, overblowing.

Overblowing was known to ancient flutists. They knew that if they forced (overblew) the wind in the flute the tone would break, jumping higher up in pitch. The new tone could likewise be raised in pitch by further overblowing. Nobody knew why this was so, but the technique was used skilfully. Both flutists and shawm-players knew when to force the wind and when to stop the finger-holes to produce the desired tone. Shepherds also played their horns this way. Overblowing became the main technique for horns and trumpets.

By skilfully manipulating their lips pressed to the cup mouthpiece, the performers could produce a whole range of sound "jumps". So, instead of a single tone, the instrument was now capable of producing a ladder of clear and ringing sounds. The sounds could be arranged tunefully to give cheerful and merry combinations.

The brazen summons of brass horns could be heard increasingly often on the chase, at knights' tournaments, and during battles. And instrument-makers adapted the brass instruments so that they suited the 'lip' technique of playing even better.

It was at that time that the mouthpiece became all-important. It was continually being re-designed and re-shaped. Every performer considered a good mouthpiece a matter of prime importance. This is not surprising, though, if we recall that a mouthpiece is also "one who speaks on behalf of others". Funnily enough, the trumpet player had come to look upon his mouthpiece as a charm; when he died, the mouthpiece went to his grave with him. This is why an ancient mouthpiece is such a rarity today. It is usually missing from the brass instruments to be found in museums. Present-day brass players are nearly as superstitious.

Gradually the 'lip' technique grew more refined and the mouthpieces more varied. The family of horns and trumpets expanded to include the post horn, the French horn (*Waldhorn* in German, meaning 'a forest horn') with its broad bell and a mellow, full tone, and the shrill narrow-tubed clarion. The ringing trumpet came by fanciful coils of thin brass tubing.

The instrument-makers worked indefatigably, urged on by the trumpeters. The compass of a dozen and a half notes was obviously not enough. Everyone was eager to invent horns and trumpets with a wider variety of tones. To meet this demand, trumpets were at one time made with additional lengths of tubing. During a performance the trumpeter would hastily insert or detach them, varying the length and thus the pitch of the note to which the instrument could be overblown. However, the performers were not happy about the business of re-making the instruments as they went along. The inventors kept looking for other devices.

In Italy in the 15th century the trumpet was developed into the trombone. In England, where it was introduced about 1500, it became known as the 'sackbut' from the French *sacqueboute* meaning 'pushpull'. It had a slide which could be extended to add various lengths of tubing for bridging the gaps in the natural, or open scale. A skilled player could move the slide quickly and precisely. By matching the movement of the slide to the work of his lips he was able to produce clear, noble sounds which wove beautifully into the 'chorus' of the orchestra. Yet it was a back-breaking job. Sometimes the hand tended to lag behind the tune, and it took much skill and a good deal of experience not to fall out of key.

The trumpet-players dreamed of a contrivance by which they could vary the length of tubing by pressing valves. Their dream came true in the early 19th century when valves were invented.

There are two types of valve, piston and rotary. In both types the valve is placed inside a cylindrical case and connected to a key which is operated by a finger. When the valve is depressed an extra length of tubing is introduced into the main tube. So there is no need for the player to insert anything or to shift anything with his hand. Only his lips and fingers are used for playing.

Whereas the ancient natural horn or clarion which depended solely on overblowing could produce only open notes, leaving gaps in the scale, the present-day valve trumpet, cornet, French horn and tuba are capable of producing a series of notes which is nearly continuous.

The brass in the present-day orchestra, with its bright and ringing voice, is used to express strong feelings: enthusiasm, festivity, triumph or, conversely, tragedy and heart-rending sorrow. And all of these sonorous and exquisite instruments are descendants of the aurochs horn, changed beyond recognition.

### THE WAY TO THE ORGAN

If the sweet-voiced flute were a braggart, it would not miss the chance of boasting of a very important and influential relative. Who do you think this relative is? It is the biggest of all the musical instruments, the organ. Difficult, as it is, to believe, both the thousand-voiced giant and the tiny flute come from the same old family.

In the old days of fairy-tales, an inventive shepherd who had grown tired of herding his cows with a single flute thought of using two at a time. No sooner said than done, and the fellow produced a double flute. But that was not enough for him. Without thinking twice he cut down half a dozen canes of different length, stopped them at one end, placed them after their length, and tied them together like a raft. This gave a new instrument which the ancient Greeks called the *syrinx*\* or Pan's pipes. Apparently, in order to be sure of success, the shrewd shepherd gave credit for the creation of the instrument to the god Pan, the mythical guardian of flocks and shepherds. This primitive instrument is still used in Oriental countries and survives in Occidental lands as a 'mouth organ'.

The earliest organ had to be played by the breath of the player blowing through the mouth as the pipes were shifted across the lips. However, more pipes were added from year to year; they were made longer and thicker to make the sound richer, and the instrument was fashioned into different forms.

The ancient Chinese invented the *sheng*, a very interesting variety of mouth organ. Imagine a large smoking pipe with a bundle

---

\* Legend attributes the origin of the instrument to the god Pan who fell in love with a beautiful nymph named Syrinx. To escape his unwelcome attentions she beseeched her sisters to change her into a cane. Pan cut down the cane, fashioned a series of pipes and played melancholy tunes on the instrument in memory of his lost love.—*Tr.*

of bamboo pipes thrust into its bowl instead of tobacco. At the lower ends the pipes each have a side-hole which is covered by a thin metal tongue or reed. As the player blows through the mouthpiece, the reeds vibrate and each pipe produces its own tone.

Incidentally, this instrument uses a fairly subtle aerodynamic mechanism. Instead of flowing from the bottom to the top, the air goes through the pipes from the top to the bottom. Strange, isn't it? How can one possibly produce a backward flowing stream of air by blowing forward? Yet, this is exactly what occurs in the *sheng*. This is because the air blown through the mouthpiece does not pass into the pipes. Instead it flows round them, producing suction in the bowl so that air is drawn into the pipes from above. The *sheng* was admitted into Chinese imperial orchestras where it was given a place of honour.

In the ancient world big Pan's pipes were also held in high esteem. But although they were pleasant to listen to, the players were in an unenviable position. Too much air had to be supplied for the now sophisticated instrument. Finally, the performers "went on strike". It's more than we can do, they said. We haven't got enough wind to blow them.

And anonymous inventors heeded their plea. They replaced the human lungs with bellows like those used to drive a strong blast of air into a blacksmith's hearth. The method of supplying wind became mechanical, giving birth to the organ. This happened five or four centuries before the present era.

The organ was to stand up to many tricks of fortune. In Byzantium it took part in solemn festivities, in Alexandria it accompanied dances, in Rome it was associated with circus performances, in Europe it was put to use by Catholic convents and churches. But even in churches, the great composers of the past made it shed ecclesiastical dejection and wake to the beauty of secular art.

All that time the organ was improving, growing more and more complicated, and gaining in strength. In the second half of the 3rd century B.C. an Alexandrian engineer named Ctesibius invented a mechanism using a water compressor and pistons to keep a constant wind-pressure in the organ. Hence the name *hydraulis,* or 'water organ'. Then followed other refinements. No other instrument has incorporated so many inventions and improvements as the organ. Nor has any other instrument reached such power and size.

This unique instrument has had many offspring, among them the "portative" or portable organ which was a scaled-down and simplified version of the stately organ, and the harmonium, also known as the cabinet organ or the American organ, which has dropped the pipes but retained the free reeds and the bellows to supply the wind.

The harmonium has given birth to a host of gleeful concertinas and harmonicas with a pair of bellows extended and collapsed by the hands, the venerable accordion, and the sonorous piano-accordion. They all come down from that giant towering above the symphony orchestra.

## A FACTORY OF SOUNDS

The organ of today is a veritable factory of sounds. In the 19th century it took a gang of hard-toiling blowers to keep the organ playing. Exerting themselves to the utmost and sweating, they worked the bellows by hand. It was not until the present century that electric motors replaced the blowers and powerful fans took the place of the bellows.

The organ is the size of a fairly large building. Its front is decorated with carved wood and the pointed pipes glimmer a dull silver. An onlooker can see only a very few of them. A big present-day organ has several thousand pipes, wooden and metal, round and square, open and stopped, narrow and wide, tall and short. Some pipes are as thick as a telegraph pole, while others are as slim as a finger. There are pipes fitted with free reeds as in the *sheng* and with beating reeds as in the clarinet. And each pipe has its own quality of tone. Wind is supplied through a system of ducts and chambers, and through a multitude of valves and slides linked to the knobs and keys on the console.

This intricate monster is controlled by the organist. He sits at the console on a long bench and operates several rows of hand keys, or the manuals, which are arranged in tiers.

Incidentally, the now familiar black-and-white keys of the piano first appeared on the organ. Originally the keys were wider than this book; they were knocked down with a blow of the fist or part of the hand, and the organist of those days was appropriately called an "organ beater". But gradually, as new mechanical contrivances were introduced, the keys were reduced in size, so that the organist could play with his fingers rather than with the whole fist. This paved the way to better fingering.

The organist not only uses his hands, though. There is another keyboard, the pedal-organ keyboard or simply the pedal-board, below the manuals. The foot-pedals are operated by the heels and toes of both feet.

And as if this were not enough there is a host of stop knobs, thumb-pistons, toe-pistons and swell-pedals to think about while playing the organ. Sometimes the organist fails to take care of everything, and assistants have to be provided. It is not surprising that many present-day organs have electrical controls. Such is the descendant of Pan's pipes, the hierarch of all wind instruments. Sheer physics and engineering: acoustics, pneumatics, electrical engineering and remote control.

The fabulous potentialities of the organ, however, more than make up for its immense complexity. It has a tonal range which even the symphony orchestra does not command. Its voice can be slow and majestically solemn, or soft and tuneful. It can be so quiet that it is hardly audible and it can be thunderous. By operating several ranks of pipes at a time the organist can produce astounding effects. The organ can sound like a brass band, like an ensemble of violins and cellos, or like a chorus. Even birds' songs can be imitated by this mammoth instrument made famous by the immortal works of Bach and Handel.

## EVOLUTION OF THE HARP

The harp looks as though it has stepped down into the orchestra from an ancient statue. Its regal bearing suggests a noble origin and many years of life in the palace.

In reality, however, it was probably invented by a prehistoric hunter, a gay and cheerful song-lover. One day as he was going back to his camp loaded with trophies he met a girl carrying a gourd vessel from a stream.

"Hello, beautiful," he said in whatever language he spoke. "Would you like me to sing a song for you?"

The girl stopped. With the radio yet to come in ten thousand years, she could not afford to miss the chance. The hunter heaved the game off his shoulders, took up his bow with two strings (one spare) and began to play a song, plucking the strings with his fingers. What he was singing about no one knows, but the girl, enchanted by the song, let the gourd fall. It rolled and stopped at the singer's feet. Playfully he stuck his bow into the vessel and plucked the strings. To his surprise the humming came out stronger. The jug seemed to have joined in the song, making it more charming.

Some time later, on their wedding day, the girl presented the lucky hunter with her gourd. He fitted it to his bow. This was the gourd bow, the primitive ancestor of the double-string lyre, which the Ethiopians call the *kissar*.

Of course, two strings were not enough; even cave musicians strived for a wider range of notes. The next step was to fit a pair of bows to the gourd. Incidentally, the African *wambee* harp is constructed this way (quite a few ancient musical instruments can be found in the Black Continent). But like the *kissar* lyre, the *wambee* harp is very crude; its strings cannot be tightened or tuned. Yet musicians were content with what little they had. It was all right as long as the *wambee* harp played, the notes were immaterial.

As the centuries passed, however, the performers improved their dexterity and the listeners grew more discerning. In what has survived as the Sudan *gunbi* harp the strings could be tensioned by winding them on a common peg with clips. The device was not particularly convenient, nor did it keep its tuning well. To make up for this the African collection contains an instrument with an excellent tuning contrivance, the *gunbi* with a peg for each string. It is easy to imagine how happy its inventor was. The separate pegs radically improved the instrument, and it became capable of many accomplishments, though it required a better technique from the performers. This modified *gunbi* came very close to the small Egyptian harp, even in shape. The Greek lyre and *kithara* were also descendants of instruments of the *gunbi* type. And the whole of this advance was due to separate pegs.

Of course, the harp of today has absorbed many other refinements that have emerged during the five thousand years of its existence. It underwent many changes as it moved from temple to temple in Egypt, from stadium to stadium in Greece, and from town to town in medieval Europe. But it was only in the last century that the harp came by its present shape. Today it has about fifty strings, foot-pedals to vary the tones of the strings, and valves in the wooden box which replaced the old gourd. The twanging of the bow-strings has changed into sparkling waves, fountains and whole waterfalls of enchanting sounds.

### SOUND-BOX, STRINGS AND NECK

A gourd or calabash for a string instrument is inexpensive and easy to obtain. And it is convenient, too. Just pick a suitable calabash in the kitchen-garden, cook and eat the fleshy part, dry the rind, and put it to some musical use. In Africa, Latin America and Asia, thousands of "singing vegetables" can be found side by side with record-players and radio sets even today.

Of course, a gourd or calabash was not the only source of material for a sound-box. The double-string Arab *rebab* used a tortoise's shell for the purpose. In one *kissar* made by Nubian man-eaters the sound-box is a human skull—a gloomy instrument to play! In all countries ancient fishermen tried seashells, and ancient potters clay jugs. Blown up pig's bladders and birch-bark boxes were also tried. Very recently the Tajik highlanders used empty cans for their instruments, some of which have even found their way into museums.

Yet, after experiments with many different materials, wood proved best. It could be made into the most ringing, the lightest and the most sensitive sound-boxes for string instruments. Way back, in ancient China and India, strings were stretched over sound-boxes fashioned from whole chunks of wood, either open or covered with a snake's skin. The ancient world and medieval Europe preferred sound-boxes with curved sides or ribs bent from thin strips of wood, a top or belly made in one or two sections and a similar back.

Many materials were tried for the strings, too: twisted bark, bamboo threads, ox's tendons, a monkey's dried intestines, or gut (even today considered best for the cello) and, of course, various wire.

Besides the sound-box and strings most string instruments also have a neck. Wood seemed the obvious choice from the outset, and instrument-makers did not have to rack their brains over it. The shape of the neck, however, caused them quite a lot of trouble.

In the African forerunners of the harp, the *kissar*, the *wambee* and the *gunbi*, the neck was steeply arched, exactly as it was in their ancestor, the bow. Many years passed before it was realized that an arched neck was not a "must".

The instrument-makers finally produced a straight neck, which was a major success. It was discovered that when the player pressed the strings down on to the smooth surface of the neck with the fingers of his left hand, the strings would produce sounds not given by free strings. Instead of a mere four or five open tones (i.e., as many as there were strings), the players now had a huge variety of them. The potentialities of performance had increased enormously.

It has never been determined where the neck was first made straight. It could have been in the *vina* of ancient India, or in the *p'i p'a* of ancient China. What is more certain is that the pressing down of strings, or finger-stopping as it is professionally termed, was first introduced in ancient Mesopotamia.

### THE FAVOURITE OF THE GALLANTS

About five thousand years ago the black-bearded Assyrians and Babylonians combined three inventions: a bulging wooden body, a broad straight neck and separate pegs for the strings. The combination was what the Arabs later named *al'ud* (wood), or the four-stringed lute.

The lute left the noisy Babylonian bazaars for Persia, India and China. In the 15th century B.C. it reached Egypt. Twenty-two centuries later it crossed the Mediterranean in company with the Moors who invaded Spain. Although the invaders failed to cross the Pyrenees to subjugate France, the peaceful lute they had brought along conquered the whole of Europe, with no resistance at all.

By that time it had changed quite a lot. Its neck had picked up a hard-wood strip, called the finger-board. Instead of pieces of rope or gut indicating where the player was to put his fingers, bone frets appeared.

The lute triumphed throughout the Middle Ages. Its voice could be heard both in palaces and at folk festivities. Gallants would not dare to express their love for a lady without it. Composers could not imagine music without the lute and even thought up a special notation for it. In brief, the lute in those days was to the Europeans what the piano is to us today.

However, its reign finally came to an end. The queen of medieval music was brought down by rivals.

The first blow came from its own offspring. Born of the lute, the simple and accessible guitar and mandolin grew up, matured and began to crowd out their distinguished mother which looked too awkward, complicated and hopelessly old-fashioned by comparison. The next blow was delivered by the bow, that dexterous substitute for the player's fingers. With this, the young violin dethroned the celebrated monarch. It couldn't be helped; every age has its own tastes.

### THE BIRTH OF A PRINCESS

Some 900 years ago an anonymous painter took great trouble to paint the frescoes in the tower of St. Sophia's Cathedral in Kiev. Apparently he was not indifferent to music and could not resist the desire to immortalize his affection on the sacred walls of the cathedral. Thus came into being the fresco showing the flutist, and another one, just as good, not far from it. The medallion shows a squatting player, with something that looks like a fiddle on his shoulder. The player draws a bow across the strings with a dashing swing.

When, many centuries later, a group of historians of the violin art visited the cathedral, they got very excited.

"Just look," some shouted. "The instrument is held on the shoulder. That's splendid indeed!"

"And the bow, look at the bow! It's as straight as a foil!" others chimed in.

Why were they so excited?

The point is that in all of the earlier pictures of bowed string instruments such as the Indian *ravanastron,* the Chinese *hu ch'in,* or the Arab *rebab,* there is not a hint that performers held them on their shoulder while playing, as present-day violinists do. Instead, the instruments were held upright, resting on the knee.

And the bow? In all of the earlier drawings, it is shown convex. The earliest straight bow (and, consequently, lighter and more flexible) is the one in the Kiev fresco. It may be added that later (in the 17th century) the concave bend, or "cambre", appeared. This was done so that when the stick was inadvertently flexed the hair would be stretched taut and not slackened.

The Kiev fresco dates back to the late 11th century, while in Western Europe similar bows did not appear in paintings until the 16th century, five hundred years later! It is not at all unlikely, therefore, that the modern way of violin playing was first used in ancient Rus.

Long ago the Southern Slavs liked to amuse themselves by "pulling a horse's hair across a sheep's gut". They handed down their primitive fiddle to West European *jongleurs,* or itinerant minstrels. In the meantime their Russian counterparts, known as *skomorokhs*, had long used the three-stringed *goudok* (known as the rebec in Western Europe) from which it was only one step to the *skrypitsa* played on the shoulder.

Unfortunately, fiddles and their like were systematically and ruthlessly destroyed in old Rus. Only on very rare occasions when the sovereign happened to be in a festive mood, would an itinerant band of *skomorokhs* be summoned to the Kremlin palace. More often the tsar's wisdom and the patriarch's sanctimony would place both fiddle makers and fiddle players on the same footing with thieves. Not infrequently the governors of the provinces and towns would receive from the tsar a decree like this: "Should domras, zournas, goudoks, gouslis, harps and any other devil's drones turn up anywhere, have your men take them away, break them and burn them." Moscow itself saw the wild destruction of musical instruments. Poor musicians would be ruthlessly banished from the city and their instruments burned by the cart-load on the outskirts.

Naturally, fiddle-makers fled from such "hospitality", while in Poland, France and Italy their number grew. There, the relatives of the Russian *goudok* came by a narrow waist like the guitar's and gave birth to the Polish *Geige,* the first established violin.

## A ROOM IN CREMONA

The violin came of age in the 18th century, in the quiet and sun-lit town of Cremona.

In the Piazza San Domenico (now the Piazza Roma) on the outskirts of that small community in northern Italy stood a three-storeyed wooden house. Right under the roof there was a room crowded with boards and blocks of wood. From the walls and ceiling hung violin necks, tops and finger-boards, and the window-sill held a supply of assorted tools and thick liquids in bottles.

It reeked of wood shavings and glue. A visitor would hear the swish of cutting-tools and knives, and see a tall lean man, wearing an apron and a white cap, bent over his bench. A simple artisan, a good husband, the father of eleven children and, it is believed, the maker of some thirteen hundred violins, violas and cellos, Antonius Stradivarius spent fifty-six years in that room. Until he died at the age of 93 he worked untiringly, turning and cutting wood, listening to its sound under the bow or a leather-encased mallet, always gluing, sawing and planing. The man possessed the astounding intuition of a scientist, the dexterity of a cabinet-maker, the sharp eye of an artist, and the perfect ear of a musician. And all of these qualities multiplied a thousand times by his inexhaustible diligence he put into his creations.

There is hardly anyone who has not heard of Stradivarius's violins. There is hardly a violinist who does not dream of playing the fabulous songstress from Cremona. Under the bow of the famous Paganini, the Cremona violin made people cry with rapture. Today, the Stradivarius violins have become valuable rarities. Only the most outstanding performers are given the honorary right to play these masterpieces.

There were also other excellent violin-makers before and at the time of Stradivarius. Among them was Giuseppe Guarneri, known as 'Joseph del Gesù', whose instruments today are the only ones considered comparable to those of Stradivarius. Other craftsmen still in very high repute are Andrea Amati, the founder of the Cremona school, Nicola Amati, his grandson and Stradivarius's teacher, and also Giovanni Paolo Maggini, the famous violin-maker of Brescia. Unique in their own right, their instruments are almost as good as the best pieces by Stradivarius.

Centuries have passed since the great Italian school came to a close. And over the centuries enraptured followers have been trying to find the secret of the Cremona masters. What is it that makes their violins so good? How do they get their tone?

## "SECRETS" OF THE OLD VIOLINS

At first, later makers thought the secret was in the shape of the instrument. After a closer look they did find that Stradivarius had his own way of making the top, the *ff*-holes, and the outline of the ribs. But there was a snag, too: out of all the known 1,150 Strads, there were no two violins with similar tops and similar tones. The shape was therefore not the main factor responsible for their excellence.

Then the investigators turned to the material. True, Stradivarius always used the best quality wood, well dried and seasoned. His choice of species was always the same, spruce for the top and maple for the back. Also, instead of working the wood into slabs, he used it in quartered form (like orange slices); that was clear from the tree rings. The makers discovered a great deal about the wood, and tried to copy what they had learned but no Stradivarius sound came. The tone of their violins was not bad, but even so it lacked something.

"This time we've got it—it's varnish!" the makers thought.

There was no denying, the varnish was excellent. Then some desperate maker risked what looked like blasphemy; he washed the varnish off a valuable Strad. And then what? After the "bath", the violin had lost its gloss and showed bald spots, but its tone remained the same.

Did the makers give up after that? Nothing of the kind. They kept on with their search. They noticed all the variations, however small and accidental. One music magazine kept the score of "findings"; every two weeks at least one lucky man somewhere in the world would declare he had hit upon Stradivarius's secret. And each time it would turn out to be an empty boast.

The perplexed makers did not know what to do. There appeared to be only one solution, to copy the famous Italians blindly and meticulously. They reasoned that if one of them made an exact copy he would at the same time discover the elusive secret. They would take apart a particularly good violin by some old master and fashion ten new ones on its pattern. They would copy every tiny knoll on the belly and back, the shape of the sound post, every curve of the *ff*-holes, and the volute of the scroll at the end of the neck. But in vain. The imitation violins were no match whatever for the wonderful original.

This time the imitators felt beaten. The art of the Cremona masters now appeared to be supernatural and beyond human capacity. There were rumours of mystics and magic.

Yet there was nothing mystical about Stradivarius and his fellow makers. Their mastery was quite down to earth.

### THE RIDDLE IS SOLVED

The old masters made no secret of their craft. Anything they made use of was there for everyone to see. Nor did they use charms or read magic words or prayers over the pieces of wood. Their success lay in their creative approach.

Stradivarius never tried to imitate anyone, nor was he particularly respectful of tradition. His only goal was to make his violin's tone beautiful and rich at any cost. Therefore, his work was that of an inexhaustible investigator. All of his violins are, in effect, studies in acoustics, and all are different. Some are more successful than others. He discovered that the quality of tone depended not so much on the various parts of the instrument as on their unity. Sometimes the slightest variation in the quality of the wood would make the old master change the outline, thickness or arch of the belly. And he would do this differently for different tones. His ear would tell him what method to follow. Of course he used his hands and eyes, but he made his violins mainly with his ears and head. Incidentally, his well-wishing neighbours used to cover the pavement near his house with hay.

It would be preposterous to ask a blind chemist to prepare good paints for a painter. Yet many a maker with no ear for music would try and produce an excuse of a violin. He would choose the material by sight, measure and mark off the parts with a pair of dividers and a rule. As he worked he never thought of the violin's tone, but treated the instrument as if it were a piece of furniture. He would use his ears only after the instrument was finished. And that was the drawback; imitation by touch and sight could not reproduce the tone of a genuine Strad. It was too sensitive and subtle for this sort of slipshod work.

Buyers, too, were to blame for the blind imitation of the old art. Hypnotized by the names of Stradivarius and Guarneri, they took no notice of the new makers. When a maker wished to earn some quick money, he would produce an exact copy (in appearance, of course) of a Cremona wonder, complete with the signature of a famous Italian. The imitation would be bought quickly and a good price would be paid. Quite a number of imitations have been sold throughout the world.

Of course, even in the darkness of imitation there were rays of genuine art. Other countries also had their talented makers, among them Ivan Batov (Count Sheremetyev's serf) and Anatoly Leman in Russia, Jacob Stainer in Germany, and Nicolas Lupot in France, to name only a few. With time, their patterns and models also came to be imitated. This was an acknowledgement of their workmanship.

Violin "counterfeiters" flourished until quite recently. Today the trade does not pay; any imitation will be identified at once. Some connoisseurs have surpassed both Sherlock Holmes and Nat Pinkerton in this art. Today almost all makers work without looking back at the past. They have realized that it is more promising to look into the future.

### FROM THE MONOCHORD TO THE CLAVICHORD

The community of musical instruments, as we have arranged them, looks rather like a monarchy, I'm afraid: the organ is the king, the harp is the queen, the lute is the queen-mother and the violin is a princess. It would be more accurate to liken them to presidents and prime ministers. For the orchestra is much more of a republic. In any case, all of its members enjoy equality of voice.

Yet, if we've taken this line, the grand piano should also be included in the musical nobility for it certainly is grand!

The piano's promotion to noble rank has been both long and difficult. Like all other instruments, it has undergone many changes and looked very humble at the bottom of its evolutionary ladder. In fact, it bore no resemblance whatsoever to the present-day grand. There was the monochord, a long wooden box with a single string stopped from beneath by a movable block. Then there was the psaltery plucked either with the fingers or with a plectrum, and the dulcimer, similar to the psaltery but struck by hammers.

At first the monochord was used as a physical instrument and a visual aid. It taught the philosophers of antiquity and medieval monks the nature of sound, which was considered a very important science.

We may well imagine that one day, either after a dull lesson or for some other reason, monastery students felt an urge for a diversion. They put together several monochords and made them play some sort of music. This, in fact, was a new instrument, a polychord. It had several strings of the same length and identically pitched. With the use of so-called tangents, which were placed under the strings at different distances, the monks were able to draw pleasant chords from it. Some suspect that Guido d'Arezzo (Guido Aretinus), who reformed musical notation, had a hand in the invention.

At that time, in the 10th century, polyphony was just beginning to find its way into church music, though performers of folk music had long used it. Many medieval fathers of the church looked upon polyphony as something sinful. "The voices of Christians in unison are more agreeable to God," they insisted.

The artful monks killed two birds with one stone by fashioning their instrument so that it could also accompany unison singing. They fitted several tangents under each string at different places and linked them to keys. When they touched the keys with their fingers, the levers beneath the strings came up, and the tangents fixed to the ends of the levers struck the strings and set them vibrating at different lengths, pouring out remarkably soft chords into the church. And so the clavichord came into being, the first keyboard instrument. No sooner had it been born, however, than it escaped from the church into secular music.

The sound of the clavichord was very soft and delicate. True, it was rather weak, but then again, it was sensitively responsive to differences of touch. By rocking the keys, the clavichord-player could make the sound last longer and vibrate. In German, it's called *Bebung,* tremor.

The unique sound of the clavichord appealed to composers. Many wrote for it. In the 18th century, after the advent of the piano, Beethoven wrote a sonata solely for the clavichord. Even today, an old clavichord is preferred when the sonata is performed. Among other merits of the clavichord were its small size and weight. Usually it was placed on a table to be played. The story goes that young Haydn, when tired of his boisterous schoolmates, would put his clavichord under his arm and run to the attic to spend hours alone with his music. Unfortunately, pianists of today cannot follow suit.

## THE GRAND HARPSICHORD

The clavichord was not alone. Growing up side by side with it was the harpsichord, the younger member of the family of keyboard instruments.

An offspring of the ancient psaltery, the harpsichord had much in common with its ancestor. The strings were of different length and arranged according to length. There were many of them, up to as many as five strings to each note or key. That was a step forward. In the clavichord each string was served by as many as four or five tangents and keys, which made it difficult to play and limited the choice of notes in a chord. It was not until the 18th century that an "unfretted" clavichord appeared with as many strings as keys.

Also, the sound was produced by a different action. Instead of the tangents, wooden uprights, or "jacks", were fitted on the rear ends of the keys. Placed on top of the jacks were raven quills. When a key was pressed, its jack jumped up, making the quill pluck the string, producing a sharp and ringing short tone. It was louder and brighter than the tone of the clavichord, but it lacked some of its quality.

On the clavichord the sound could, within narrow limits, be varied in strength and made to last longer, but there was no way of doing this on the harpsichord. Whatever the strength of a stroke, the quill plucked the string in the same way.

Yet the sound of the harpsichord deserved admiration. Fresh and sparkling as rain-drops in the sun, it won many followers. Even today Mozart's *Alla Turca* calls for a harpsichord. In fact, it was written for the instrument.

It is not surprising, therefore, that the harpsichord outgrew its melancholy elder brother and literally rose to its own feet.

It also changed in shape. The square design of the clavichord gave way to the winged construction of the present-day grand. In the grand harpsichord the strings were stretched on a strong wooden frame over a thin wooden soundboard which absorbed the sound to reradiate it in a broad stream up and down.

Minor improvements followed one after another. The quill claw gave way to a leather or metal plectrum and the gut strings were replaced by metal wires. All this added strength and colour to the tone of the instrument.

Despite all these devices, however, the main drawback of the harpsichord, the lack of tonal flexibility, stubbornly persisted.

Quite a number of ingenious things were devised to cover it up, among them additional keyboards or manuals as in the organ, each plucking the strings in its own way and producing tones of different colour. In this way the harpsichord was made to imitate the lute and the harp. Then more strings were added, among them a set of unison strings which could be plucked two, three or even four at a time. There was also a lever which pressed a strip of paper down onto the strings, producing the wheeze of the bassoon.

With the sophistication of two or even three keyboards the harpsichord grew more and more difficult and costly to make. The makers were lavish in decorating it so as to lure the rich into paying. Bright, multi-coloured pictures were drawn on its body and cover, and the wood was given a mirror polish. Their plan worked; the instrument looked exactly what the nobility was after.

Sporting its exquisite attire with an air of dignity and importance, the harpsichord certainly looked smart. It settled firmly into aristocratic drawing-rooms both as a piece of fashionable furniture and as a refined musical instrument. Composers had learned how to exploit its remarkable potentialities to the utmost. Its tone, now softly sharp, light and fluttering, and now austere, ringing and metallically abrupt, was an attractive antithesis to the ponderous ecclesiastical dignity of the organ.

As time passed, however, musicians became accustomed to the merits of the harpsichord and were eager to have what it could not give them, a sustained and infinitely graduated tone, and greater tonal volume and beauty. In spite of all its contrivances, the harpsichord did not develop any of these refinements.

### AN ENDLESS BOW

For years man dreamed of an instrument which would encompass a whole orchestra. One of the earliest ideas dates back to well before the birth of the harpsichord. It originated with Leonardo da Vinci, the great Italian scientist, engineer, painter and musician.

In 1490 Leonardo da Vinci planned a keyboard instrument which would use a friction action as in the violin, instead of the hammer action of the dulcimer or the plectrum of the psaltery.

He imagined an instrument with revolving wheels whose rims would be rubbed with rosin. When the player pressed a key, the rosined rim would set the string vibrating. The wheel "bow" would pull across the string until the key was released. The note would be long and steady. By playing chords, it would be possible to imitate an ensemble of bowed string instruments!

But this intriguing project was not realized by Leonardo da Vinci himself. An instrument looking very similar to his plan, however, was built by Hans Hayden of Nuremberg some time later. Today, the instrument has been forgotten. Apparently its tone was not very pleasant, for it is more difficult to draw a good tone with a bow than with a plectrum or a hammer. Also, in addition to the player, there must be an assistant to rotate the wheels all the time, like millstones. Yet da Vinci's idea has survived in the hurdy-gurdy and the small wheel lyres, folk instruments which you can still find in many countries.

Other schemes have also been tried. In some, different instruments would be combined mechanically so as to be sounded by a hammer action, say, a harpsichord, cymbals, drums and kettledrums. Sometimes, even flutes and trumpets would be added. Of course, such musical

*An ancient Egyptian fresco showing a harpist*

Krishna playing a flute (an ancient Indian fresco)

Playing a lyre (a Grecian vase)

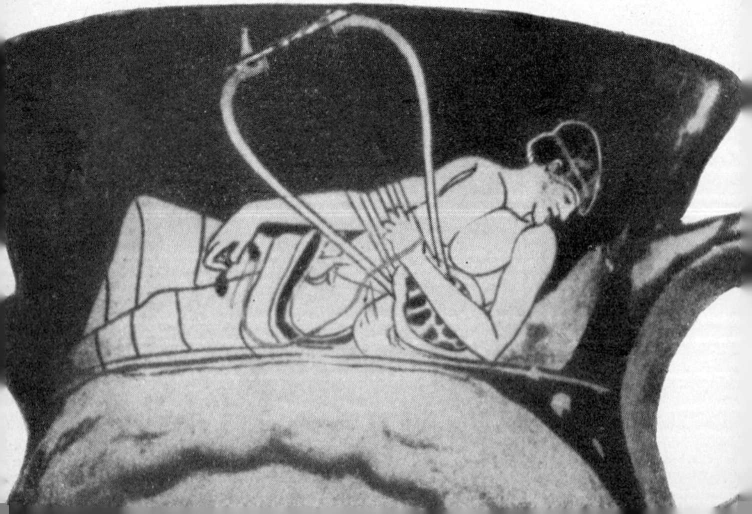

"The Skomorokhs." A fresco on the Southern Tower of St. Sophia's Cathedral in Kiev. 11th century

*A detail of the fresco "The Musicians" on the Northern Tower of St. Sophia's Cathedral in Kiev. 11th century*

*"A Gousli-player." A detail of the fresco "The Performance of Skomorokhs", from Adam Olearius's "Journey to Muscovia", 17th century*

mongrels were too complicated and inconvenient to play.

Sometimes extremely strange instruments would appear. One such instrument, which has remained an enigma till today, was the Golden Dionysus made by Prokopy Divish in the early 18th century. According to contemporary records the instrument had 790 strings and permitted 130 gradations of tone. It is said to have been equipped with some electrical devices.

More ideas were suggested as more attempts failed. Instrument-makers turned out one model after another. However history, that exacting connoisseur, has chosen and preserved only one of them. It is the piano, so well known and popular today.

**PIANO E FORTE**

The man who handed down to us the violin as we know it today has been made immortal in proverbs, legends and books. By contrast, the inventor of the piano is known only to historians of music, who do not know very much either. History has not given him his fair share of fame, although his contribution was large.

Bartolommeo Cristofori, an Italian, was the custodian of a collection of musical instruments in Florence. He had spent all his life among harpsichords and was always looking for new improvements in their design. He was an excellent harpsichord-maker, and was sceptical about the gigantism which was beginning to affect keyboard instruments at that time. He felt he should find something simple and fundamentally new. However, the invention which was to become great matured in his mind only in the evening of his life.

His idea was simple. Instead of plucking the strings as in the harpsichord or pressing them as in the clavichord, they could be conveniently struck with hammers. The strength of the blow could be controlled, and so could the tone.

The idea was not new, though. It was already used in the ancient dulcimer. The problem was to match the strength of the blow of the hammer to the pressure on the key. A strong blow on the string should result from heavy pressure on the key, and vice versa. This was the main thing.

No one knows how many nights Cristofori spent without sleep, looking for the best embodiment of his idea. No one knows how many designs were discarded before he produced what he thought good.

Finally he fitted each key with an ingenious double leverage of wood, which terminated in a light leather-encased hammer. The hammer struck the string, and a soft felt damper stopped it as soon as the key was released.

In 1709 Cristofori exhibited four harpsichords with hammer action. The inventor called them *gravicembalo col piano e forte*—harpsichords with soft and loud tone. Those were the authentic forerunners of today's pianoforte.

The instruments were shown to Prince Ferdinando dei Medici, Cristofori's patron, and in 1711 were described by Scipione Maffei in his

*Giornale dei litterati d'Italia*. But in spite of the advantages of the pianoforte, musicians did not accept it overnight, and Cristofori died a poor man in 1731.

Although Italy invented the piano, the first to make it commercially was Gottfried Silberman, the famous German organ-builder. He adopted Cristofori's action and built the best pianoforte he could. But when he asked Johann Sebastian Bach to play it, the great musician criticized its weak treble and heavy action. It is rumoured that after Bach's departure the temperamental master chopped up the instrument with an axe. Eventually he perfected it and Frederick the Great of Prussia bought three of them. They are now in Potsdam palaces.

**THE GRAND PIANO**

Cristofori died in obscurity. He did not live to see the brilliant triumph of his invention. To many, the loud and clear tone of the piano sounded unrefined and harsh. Even in the 19th century the new instrument had opponents, and not only among ignoramuses. Heinrich Heine disliked it, for example. He considered it blasphemy to strike the strings with hammers.

Fortunately, the final word lay with the musicians and not the poets. The piano won the approval of Bach, Mozart and Beethoven. Its volume and variety of tones made it welcome in large orchestras. The public came to like its beautiful and sonorous tone which was unlike anything that had existed before. It could rise to a peal of thunder and then drop to a hardly audible *pianissimo*. The grand became the working instrument for composers and found its way into the homes of townspeople. The art of piano playing developed in big strides. A galaxy of pianists, headed by Liszt, won the same renown as the most celebrated singers and violin-players.

This great success inspired piano-makers to make even better instruments, and the grand of today is the outcome of the effort of many generations.

Cristofori's piano is now highly refined. The slightest variation in the pressure on its keys is faithfully reproduced as the finest shading of tone. The grand is never choked by even the most rapid *tremolo*.

A very important step forward came with the introduction of the pedals, especially the damper pedal which keeps the dampers off all the strings. This pedal has given the grand an additional capacity to sustain and combine tones, to enrich chords, and to control the tone colour.

There have been changes in the strings as well. They have become both stronger and more attractive. Brass is no longer used; it has been replaced by a special grade of steel which is thoroughly worked. More strings have been added and their tension increased, since this improves their sound.

What do you think is the total tension of the strings on the frame of a grand? Thirty tons weight! The wooden case of the early grand would snap at once. These days, therefore, it is reinforced with a cast-iron framework.

Instead of a single row of strings as in the early grand, they are now arranged in two or even three rows in a criss-cross manner. This arrangement saves space without reducing the length of the strings.

The soundboard was re-designed in the early grand pianos. It became thinner, stronger and more resounding than that of the harpsichord. This is how Mozart expressed his admiration of the way the famous piano-maker Johann Stein of Augsburg used to construct his soundboards: "When he makes one, he exposes the board to the air, the sun, the rain and the snow, for all the devils to play havoc with it, until it cracks all over. Then, using strips and glue, he fills up the cracks. When thus made, you may be sure the soundboard will stand up to anything."

Nowadays the soundboard is the subject of a good deal of scientific research. Treatises are being written on its material, thickness, dimensions and configuration. As the acoustical heart of the grand it certainly deserves this attention.

Many makers have tried to re-style the piano in a more radical way. They have put it on end, or joined two grands together, or re-designed the keyboard. None of these schemes has come to stay with us, however, except the upright piano invented in 1880 and now favoured everywhere. As for the grand, including automatic and electric models, the time-proven Cristofori principle still holds good. Now, 150 years after his death, a monument has at last been set up to this outstanding man at Padua, his home town.

The grand piano completes our journey into the history of musical instruments, a journey as brief and superficial as that of foreign tourists on a week's tour of a big country. But we have been able to point out one very important feature, the close union between musicians and instrument-makers. Every new instrument has appeared in response to the needs of the performers, thus opening a new page in the history of music. The lute, the violin, the organ, the harpsichord and the piano have each marked an epoch in the musical history of Europe.

We have also noticed that the road leading to the modern orchestra has been long and thorny. At first, man did not even know what sound was, nor why was it produced or changed. Much time and effort was wasted. Discoveries were made by accident, while groping blindly in the dark.

But finally the day came when science held out a helping hand to music.

CHAPTER TWO

✳

# How Sound Is Produced

What is the strongest thing in the world? What is the fastest? What is the sweetest? In fairy-tales the characters have to rack their brains to solve these riddles.

The reader is also asked a riddle: what is the softest thing in the world?

You may think a down-bed? Or a pillow? No, the answer is air.

Yes, air. It is softer and more yielding than down. Inflated mattresses are best.

Well, and what is most elastic?

Neither springs nor rubber, but again air. Although soft, it is extremely elastic. Otherwise you would not inflate your football with air, for the ball would refuse to spring, as if stuffed with cotton wool.

At one time the elasticity of "super-soft bodies", gases, amazed physicists and sparked off many heated debates. The puzzling question was answered by Mikhail Lomonosov of Russia. The enigmatic elasticity was found to be due to the random motion of gas molecules. Striking the wall of the vessel holding a gas, they build up pressure which stubbornly resists compression.

So the world we live in is immersed in a huge elastic ocean. This is why it is full of sounds.

When you clap your hands, a volume of air is rapidly compressed. Because of its elasticity, it expands again at once to compress an adjacent volume of air. This air also tends to expand again and so an invisible wave moves on and on. On reaching your ear it strikes the ear-drum, and you feel what we call sound.

In short, sound is an elastic wave travelling through air. This has been known to man since ancient times. Two thousand years ago the Roman architect Vitruvius described the propagation of sound so accurately that the most exacting of physics teachers today would give him full marks.

What interests us, however, is not just any sound, but only musical sounds.

Experts say that a wolf's howl and a mosquito's drone are both musical sounds, while the beat of a drum and the rattle of castanets are simply noises.

Drummers, of course, are indignant, but that cannot be helped. Such is science's verdict. It classes as musical sounds only those which are identified with a recognizable pitch. Because of this, a locomotive's whistle shares the poetical company of the violin.

Yet how does a sound become musical? How does it come by its pitch? It is very simple. The elastic waves of air must travel in a definite order and not in a random manner. When a steady train of waves following each other at regular intervals passes through the air, your ear hears a continuous sound of a definite pitch. As the waves grow more frequent, they become shorter in length, and the sound rises in pitch from the lowest to the highest tone. This rise in frequency and pitch deserves special mention.

### UP AND DOWN THE SOUND LADDER

Some thirty years ago, a London theatre planned to stage a play in which the action takes place way back in the past. The stage director thought it would be a good idea to put in some effect to give a flavour of antiquity. But which effect to use? Light effects would be too common, and music would drown the actors' voices. So he took advice from Wood, a physicist, who suggested that he use infra-sound, that is sound lying below the audibility range of man. Wood insisted that it would produce a feeling of mystery if it were sufficiently strong.

The scientist made a source of infra-sound, a huge organ pipe. It was tried at a rehearsal. A newsman who was there recalls, "the effect was unexpected, like an earthquake; the window-panes rattled, the glass chandeliers jingled. The whole of the old building quivered, and terror swept the audience. Even the people in adjacent houses panicked."

Scared out of his wits, the director told the stage hands to throw out the "damned thing" at once.

That was the only known attempt to use infra-sound in the arts. However, it serves science faithfully. There are instruments which are sensitive to infra-sound. Geophysicists use them to forecast storms at sea and to study earth tremors.

The lowest musical sound man can hear has a frequency of 16 vibrations per second. It is produced by the organ. However, it is seldom used as it is too low and difficult to catch.

The tone of frequency 27, although also rare, is easy for the human ear to catch. You will hear it if you press the key on the far left of the piano.

Another interesting tone, with 44 vibrations per second, is the lowest sound ever produced by male voice. The "record" was set by the singer Caspar Fesper in the 18th century. Today Norman Allin of Britain can produce it.

Let us climb steadily up the sound ladder. Here is a tone of frequency 80. It is the lowest limit for an ordinary good bass and for many instruments. If we double the frequency (by going up an octave) we obtain a tone which is within the reach of the cello and the viola. The bass, the baritone, the tenor and the contralto all feel comfortable with it.

Another octave up and we find ourselves in a range swarming with music. Nearly all voices and musical instruments can produce tones in this range. This is why today's standard concert pitch has been pinned at frequency 440—the A of the treble clef. This note is regularly transmitted over the radio in the Soviet Union and elsewhere for tuning. It is a sort of peg which keeps the sound ladder arranged in a recognizable manner, so that it can be used for tuning, playing, and music-writing.

The audio range is full of music up to frequencies 1,000-1,200. These sounds are the most audible. Those above them are accessible only to the violin, the flute and such versatile instruments as the pipe organ, the piano and the harp. The bright soprano, however, is quite at home in this range.

In fact, the female voice can reach even higher. In the 18th century Mozart was enraptured by Lucrezia Agujari, an Italian operatic soprano whose compass extended to C *in altissimo* (frequency 2,018). The French soprano Madot Robin (who died in 1960) could sing as high as D *in altissimo* (frequency 2,300) at full volume.

Add to this a few little-used steps, perhaps reached only by whistle-performers, and the musical range is exhausted. Sounds above frequencies 2,500-3,000 are never used as independent musical tones. They have a harsh and screaming quality about them. Would any composer write music consisting of whistles and a mosquito's drone?

Above frequencies 16,000-20,000 comes ultrasound, which consists of sound waves too frequent to be heard. However, it is used for quite a number of jobs: it drills stone, removes rust, grinds materials, washes linen, measures the depth of rivers and seas, and detects flaws in parts better than X-rays. And it does all this silently.

## SWEET-VOICED DEVICES

Now we have learned how sound is produced and what musical sounds are like. We have realized that all their lives musicians simply make the air vibrate, quickly or slowly, violently or only slightly. And their instruments, which have been perfected over thousands of years, serve exactly this purpose.

This brings us to the working of musical instruments.

According to an encyclopaedia, any musical instrument is simply "a physico-acoustical contrivance" which imparts various combinations of oscillatory motion to the surrounding air. Apparently, a singer's vocal cords also fall into this category.

Some readers may not be very happy about this definition. It does not become the royal violin to be called a physico-acoustical contrivance, they might say. However, there is no option; this is how things are. If a romanticist or a poet wishes to get to their essence, he will have to learn to look at them in a different way.

To physicists, a musical instrument is a combination of a vibrator and a resonator. If we are to understand the physical nature of music, we will have to learn what these two things are.

Let us begin with vibrators. There are many of them around us. The swing-boat at fairs is a vibrator. The pendulum of a clock is a vibrator. A door spring is a vibrator. Science gives this name to anything which can be set vibrating by an impact, a blow, or friction.

If the vibrations are frequent, coming at a rate of tens, hundreds, or thousands per second, the vibrator sends out sound waves through the air, and it is called an acoustical vibrator. This is where all music, instrumental and vocal, is born physically.

An acoustical vibrator must be elastic. You cannot make one from soft wax. Metal or cane tongues, stretched films, gut or wires all make excellent acoustical vibrators. They are fitted into wind instruments, violins, or drums. Some musical instruments consist solely of vibrators. These include the xylophone, the gong, bells and cymbals. When a singer is singing, his vocal cords act as vibrators.

The string is the most common vibrator, and it deserves a closer look to see how it works.

An impatient reader may ask why we are wasting so much time on such simple things. What can be simpler than a vibrating string? Just strike or pluck it, and that is all there is to it.

Do not be in such a hurry. As often as not, things that appear to be very simple turn out to be a real puzzle. Quite a number of physicists and mathematicians have worked on the secrets of the string.

Much of what we know today about its none-too-easy theory is due to Thomas Young, a brilliant British scientist who lived in the late 18th and the early 19th century. His life and work are the first we shall look into. So, I invite you to the circus of a hundred years ago.

## THE PHYSICIST ON A ROPE

Every evening Fraconi's Circus is flooded with light. A fast horse with an elegant rider on its back appears in the arena. Standing on the saddle, the rider greets the spectators and thrills them with his acrobatics. Then he jumps up from the horse, climbs a long rope like a cat and, keeping his balance with smooth movements of his hands, dances over the heads of the enraptured people. The deft performer wins enthusiastic applause. He takes several curtain calls and receives flowers.

An hour later he can be seen in his study, among books and physical instruments, poring over a sheet of paper covered with mathematical formulae. A virtuoso of the tightrope, he is busy formulating the theory of the string, its smaller counterpart.

The acrobat-scientist was Thomas Young, an amazing man whose motto was: "Anyone can do what others do." Sticking to this hard rule, he learned many trades besides that of a circus performer. He was an admirer of painting, and knew all the fine techniques of artists. As if this were not enough, he was a musician and could play nearly all of the instruments of his time.

As a boy of two, Young learned to read. At five, a Bristol professor taught him literature. At seven, he had a good command of trigonometry and geodesy. Between the ages of nine and fourteen, he studied the ancient classics, picked up five foreign languages, and learned to operate a lathe and to use the differential calculus.

At 18, as a medical student, he made quite a stir in the scientific world with his work on the physiology of vision. Then papers and investigations began to come in a flood. Young worked on Egyptian hieroglyphics, edited a shipping calendar, wrote sixty scientific entries for the Encyclopaedia Britannica, published his works on mechanics, optics, the theory of elasticity, acoustics, heat, shipbuilding, astronomy, geophysics, medicine, zoology and a host of other things.

Young's career, sparkling as a many-faceted crystal, has been described in many books. We shall only dwell on one of his contributions to science, his epoch-making discovery of the interference of waves.

The basic idea of Young's discovery is simple. When two trains of waves meet, they alternately add together and subtract from each other. As a result, in addition to the original, "bigger" waves and "smaller" waves are produced. They can all co-exist in the same vibrator. Therefore almost any vibrator produces several frequencies. This is best exemplified by the stretched string.

### MANY TONES FROM A SINGLE STRING

In the daytime, the circus was deserted. After his Egyptian hieroglyphics, Young could switch over to his acrobatics and entertain himself with physical experiments at the same time.

He would walk along the rope and jump down, making the rope vibrate like a big string. He could see a long, lazy wave rise and fall between the posts. In the middle the swing was greatest. Physicists call it a loop or an antinode.

Young would go to the winch and stretch the rope tighter. The swings would become more rapid because of the closer coupling between the rope particles which could now transmit motion quicker. The same result is obtained with a shorter rope, since vibrations travel faster through it. Everything looked so ordinary and familiar. However, if the physics of the rope were as simple as that, the violin and the guitar would not play as they do. Their tones would be dull and colourless.

Young would strike the rope again and throw back his head, looking for proof of the interference principle he had postulated. Finally, he found it.

If you look closely at a swinging rope you will notice not one but several "standing" waves. This is because the rope vibrates simultaneously in several ways. In the first place, it vibrates as a whole. Then there are two more waves each half the rope's length, riding the main wave. They are separated by a node, a relatively stationary point looking like a clamp on the rope. Then there are three waves each covering a third of the rope's length, also separated by nodes and with a loop or antinode at the middle of each third. The same is true of the rope's fourths, fifths, etc. Theoretically, a vibrating rope can be divided into any integral number of equal, or aliquot, parts.

Thus, a long vibrating body is not the smooth arc it appears at first glance. At any moment, it is wriggling in intricate turns and is studded with an array of standing waves which are both independent of, and penetrate, one another.

The string behaves exactly the same way. The only difference is that the rope swings slowly and therefore silently, while the rapid vibrations of the string produce an audible sound. In fact, it is not a single tone but a whole series, each part of the string adding its own tone.

Thus it turns out, quite unexpectedly, that a single string gives out a chorus of tones. This is the secret of the violin's and the guitar's beautiful performance.

### THOMAS YOUNG'S LAWS

Human voices are accurately graded and each has a name of its own: the bass, the baritone, the tenor, etc.

The order is as strict for the tones of the string.

Vibration of the entire length of the string gives the fundamental tone, or the first harmonic. It is the loudest of all. The string's halves give a tone an octave higher, since they vibrate twice as quickly. Their tone is called the 1st overtone or the 2nd harmonic. The string's thirds produce the still higher 2nd overtone or the 3rd harmonic, its fourths produce the 3rd overtone or the 4th harmonic, and so on.

A chorus leader controls his singers smoothly. At a movement of his hand, the basses stop and the sopranos sing louder. At another, the baritone comes in, accompanied by the trebles. At a third movement, only the solo tenor can be heard.

Can the string's chorus be controlled in any way? Yes, it can.

When the string is plucked suddenly, rapid and short standing waves are produced in it. When it is pulled softly, the waves are slow and long. Because of this, high overtones can be heard in the former case, and low ones in the latter case. This is why the mandolin played with a plectrum gives out clear and sharp tones, while those of the guitar are softer and deeper.

The point at which the string is excited is also important. Indeed, it makes all the difference where the string is struck or bowed.

Young's first law states: you cannot excite a standing wave by vibrating its node. To put it differently, if the tone is to be bright and ringing, strike the string at one of its ends. Then you will not run the risk of striking at a node common to a large number of energetic standing waves; both low and high overtones will chime in. The fundamental tone will be reinforced by a good number of rejoicing "boys' voices". As the point where the bow is drawn or the plectrum strikes moves farther away from the ends of the string, overtones become progressively fewer.

If a string is excited at its middle point a good proportion of its harmonics are lost since this point is the node common to all the odd overtones, beginning with the first one. None of them can be brought to life.

Now it is not difficult to understand the reason why instruments with strings excited at the middle are a rare occurrence, although they are easier to set vibrating. It is not always possible, though, to place the striking points near the ends of a string; it is difficult to set a string vibrating near the pegbox or the stringholder. It takes a strong blow to excite it. Only when stretched taut and therefore elastic, can strings be excited at the ends. In some of the modern makes of piano which have strong and taut-stretched strings, the hammers strike near the ends of the strings. The sound is therefore full, bright and sonorous.

Young's second law states: a node of standing waves is formed at the point where a vibrating string is stopped. Although they may be unaware of it, violinists have been making use of this law for a long time. By pressing the string lightly at the nodes of the aliquot parts (thirds, fourths, fifths, etc.), they can draw flute-like, or flageolet, tones from the violin. With this technique, the higher overtones are bolstered, while the lower harmonics are suppressed. It is as if someone had put gags into the mouths of all the singers in a choir except for a few selected soloists.

Today, physics has got down to the fundamentals of how a string works. What once was discovered through intuition and trial and error can today be accomplished by precise calculation. The slide-rule has become as important to instrument-makers as their traditional tools. They have inherited Young's formulae which save much time and effort.

That is about all we need to know about the string, a member of the large family of musical vibrators.

Next comes the second aspect of the musical instrument as a "physico-acoustical contrivance". This is the resonator.

### MUSICAL VESSELS

One day a company of soldiers was marching on a bridge. The soldiers were marching as one, keeping step with each other. All of a sudden the bridge fell apart like a house of cards.

You must have heard this instructive story and probably know the cause of its sad outcome, resonance.

What is resonance? Every physical system, including bridges, has a natural frequency of vibration. If such a system is given impulses with a frequency approaching the natural frequency, its response (or swing) increases many times as exact synchronism is reached. That is resonance.

The bridge collapsed because the rhythm of the soldiers' steps coincided with its natural frequency of vibration; the bridge's swings became too much for its strength, and it "snapped".

The bridge thus acted as a resonator, or a device reinforcing the original vibrations. Music uses quite a number of such devices, though with a more pleasant effect.

I hope instrumentalists will not be offended if I liken many of them to cooks. No kitchen can do without pots or pans. In music, too, every instrument is a vessel. In a wind band, music is "cooked" in pipes and tubes; in a stringed orchestra this is done in boxes.

Of course, musical vessels are more complicated and diverse than kitchen utensils. They may be open or closed, and made of wood or metal. The quality of musical "meals" depends very much on them. Even a slight flaw in an instrument may spoil the "dish". If a violin has its bottom missing the result is much the same as for a tureen; music will "run out" and be wasted. Incidentally, there is one use for "bottomless" silent violins. Violinists "play" them to practise without being a nuisance to their neighbours.

What, then, are sound vessels and why are they so important? They are resonators, i.e., devices which reinforce the sounds produced by vibrators.

The sound produced by strings or reeds is hardly audible. It is weak and excites a limited volume of air. The vibrations of strings or reeds can only be transmitted to larger bodies of air by fitting resonators, "acoustic levers" in the form of wooden or metal cases, bellies, soundboards, tubes, and so on.

How do they work?

This question was answered by Hermann von Helmholtz, the German scientist of world renown, who reached the peak of his career in the latter half of the 19th century.

Salieri, whom legend at one time held responsible for Mozart's death by poison, says in Pushkin's drama

> ........I slew
> The sounds and, like a corpse, dissected them
> And tested their harmony with algebra....

It would be more appropriate to give credit for this to the well-wishing genius of Helmholtz. A man of exceptional versatility, Helmholtz was prominent in many branches of physics, medicine, and the physiology of the sensory organs. He was the first to study resonators, to analyze the spectrum of musical sounds, to unravel the secret of timbre, to formulate a theory of the human voice and hearing, and to put musical harmony on a mathematical footing.

Helmholtz was one of those lucky scientists who live to win general recognition. His experiments were repeated and confirmed in dozens of laboratories. Physicians, engineers and musicians were eager to make him a member of their societies. Kings gave him decorations. Medals were coined and scholarships established in his honour. He was given a magnificent welcome in Berlin, Vienna and St. Petersburg.

However, he lacked simple human happiness in his family life. His wife died young; his son, a talented engineer and his pride and hope, was killed in an accident; his son by a second marriage was an imbecile.

To make up for all this, he drew strength and joy from his work, and was selfless and purposeful.

He had a keen eye for riddles and problems in things other people considered obvious and routine. He never missed a chance to get to the roots of the unexplained, and did so with devotion.

### A CRICKET ON THE HEARTH

Feeling tired after a day's work, Helmholtz went to his bedroom, undressed and blew out the candle when he heard a cricket. An ordinary cricket, the old symbol of a cosy home, struck up its song. The scientist forgot his tiredness, sat up in bed and listened. He listened in his own way, as a physicist, immediately planning how to analyze this chance sound for its frequency spectrum and timbre. He folded a piece of cardboard into a tube and inserted it into his ear. Aha! The sound was now muffled —apparently the air in the tube did not resonate in sympathy with the night guest's song. He made a second and then a third tube. In moonlight, on a scrap of paper, he computed the natural frequency of the improvized resonator. He thought hard and finally arrived at a conclusion. His observation of the cricket was later included in his famous book *On the Sensations of Tone as a Physiological Basis for the Theory of Music*.

The range of experiments described in this monumental work is amazing. First come the simplest "musical vessels", hollow balls and stopped brass tubes. The elastic bodies of air inside them vibrate in the simplest way, without any overtones. In bigger balls the vibrations grow more slowly and the "clear tone" becomes deeper.

In his experiments Helmholtz arranged the resonating balls in a long row on a table. They were all of different sizes, each smaller than the next. They were the "listeners"; a violinist, a trumpeter, or a flutist played in front of them.

As the musician played, Helmholtz put his ear to each ball in turn. Some remained silent, and some resonated. Since the natural frequencies of the resonators were known, the experimentor could easily identify the clear tones in the mixture of sounds. Thus the "recipe" of the timbre, or tone colour, could be made out. That was how tonal spectra were first obtained, and music itself was "taken apart".

Helmholtz built some clever devices for keeping track of vibrations. He tested and tried a multitude of sounds and their combinations. His experiments confirmed all that the tireless Young had learned about the string. In all cases too many lower overtones would make the sound soft, deep, round and warm, while too many higher overtones would produce a bright, clear and sharp tone colour.

Sound was not only tested but also explained with increasing detail and understanding. While Young had described a typical vibrator, the string, Helmholtz formulated a mathematical theory for a typical resonator, the organ pipe. The ingenious method he used has been serving engineers ever since. He learned how to blend the tones of tuning forks to give composite musical sounds like those of the flute and the trumpet. He could even produce the vowels of human speech. His tuning forks could "say" a's, o's, i's and u's.

Helmholtz's investigations clarified the basic physics of musical vessels.

### AIR IS LIKE A STRING

The basis of any resonator is the body of air it contains. This was proved by Helmholtz. We know that air is elastic. Naturally, the columns of air "poured" into the tubes of horns, flutes, trumpets and trombones are also elastic. And a long elastic body behaves like a string.

Of course, there are some differences. A string vibrates transversely, and air lengthwise; a column of air is more like a long helical spring. Also, the air string is much lighter than one made of steel; it vibrates more rapidly and comes to a stop sooner. Because of this, a single impulse cannot keep it vibrating. On the other hand, it will respond to continuous agitation with steady natural vibrations. In this way the air column reinforces the scarcely audible sound of the vibrator through resonance.

When a flutist blows his flute, the air column is agitated to give out its natural, or fundamental, tone. As the player stops the fingerholes, the length of the "string" changes, and so does the pitch of the flute. If the flutist blows harder, the "string", instead of vibrating full length, vibrates in its halves, and we hear our old acquaintance, the 1st overtone. With a still stronger blast the air column vibrates in thirds, fourths, and so on, so that the 2nd, and then the 3rd and higher overtones appear. This is overblowing, the most common technique in playing all wind instruments.

However, the overtones in resonators have to "cut their coats according to their cloth". In the simple flute there is too little room for standing waves to show themselves, and the variety is limited. The oboe and the bassoon with their expanding tubes can "cook" a richer mixture of overtones. As for the clarinet, there is even a sort of 'wind flageolet tone' to be heard. The tube of the clarinet has a hole one-third of the way along its length, through which the air column comes into slight contact with the atmosphere. When the hole is opened, the odd partials are eliminated, and a peculiar tone colour is obtained.

All of the woodwind instruments have one feature in common—their tubes are vessels in the direct, non-musical sense of the word. They cannot vibrate and are only there to contain air. They may therefore be made of any material which is sufficiently strong, light and easy to work. Also, they are almost as easy to design as a string.

With the brass instruments, things are different. The walls of their tubes also give out their own tones. The sound of the trumpet and the French horn is in fact a duet between the metal and the air column, a duet which is not at all easy to treat mathematically. It was not until the last few decades that scientists worked out an acoustical theory of wind resonators and suggested the best forms for them.

The thin-walled resonating bodies of stringed instruments, however, are the most complex of all. Just as all roads lead to Rome, any talk about musical instruments eventually converges on the violin. Our talk is no exception.

CHAPTER THREE

✳

# Rivals of Stradivarius

Why is it that the violin is not round like, say, the banjo? Because it is made of wood.

Wood is grainy in structure. And sound travels faster along the grain than across it. The violin, the guitar, the mandolin and their relatives have their body made from boards cut lengthwise so that the sound can take the same time to travel in both directions.

As a rule, the ratio of the length of a violin to its width is the same as the ratio of the velocity of sound along the belly to that across it. When this ratio is accurately observed, the wooden resonator works best. Then the belly flexes up and down equally along and across the grain, and the resonator has the greatest swing, vibrating as a single whole. This ratio can only be found through experiments, which thus become vitally important.

Of course, this ratio is not everything. Especially when it comes to making a violin.

The body of a violin is a delicate thing. It is not flat; it is both bent and arched. The sound of the air inside the body is added to that of the wood, and what we hear is a "duet between wood and gas".

Numerous "air strings" vibrate inside the body of a violin, making a well-fitting assembly of millions of flutes, of different length and bore, open and stopped. Together they take part in a very complex and involved acoustic process. Because of this complexity, physicists have as yet failed to produce a comprehensive theory of the violin resonator, in spite of all their efforts.

But work has been done on such a theory, and there is something to show for it.

### SAVART'S COFFIN

It was in the early 19th century. Félix Savart, a young physician in Strasbourg, liked physics and music more than medicine. He was an enthusiastic admirer of the violin and the first to look upon it as a physical device and to call its delicate body "a resonator", a new word at that time and a blasphemous one to any musician.

Somehow or other he came by a Strad and carried out all sorts of experiments on it. He removed the strings, tapped at the violin's arched belly with his fingers as though it were a patient, blew into it as if it were a flute and pasted wooden blocks to the body here and there and listened to their sound.

Savart concluded from his acoustic experiments that the Cremona violin was a tuned resonator. When tapped or blown, even without strings, it gave the same tone—middle C of the pianoforte. What he had discovered was a very important feature of a good violin.

But the various parts of the resonator sounded differently. The bridge, the back, the belly and the sound post each had a tone of its own. Like the string, the resonator was made up of a chorus.

After his discovery, Savart asked himself whether the same chorus could be reproduced in some other form of resonator? Was the classical shape of the Italian violin with its arches, rounded bouts and waist a "must"?

More experiments followed. Savart traced the passage of sound waves in wooden blocks, noticing how they changed in going from one part to another. He determined the frequency of sound waves by using the recently invented steam siren and also established, for the first time, the limit of audibility.

In the end Savart concluded that the beauty of Cremona had an ideally shaped body. Centuries of trials and rejections had not been wasted. Even a small patch over the *ff*-holes or a slight shift in the position of the bridge would change the sound beyond recognition. Yet Savart made an attempt to improve the resonator.

The scientist made a drawing of his own violin and had Jean-Baptiste Vuillaume, the famous Paris violin master, make a violin to his drawing. It was easy to make. It had neither smoothly curved bouts nor a waist, and the *ff*-holes were straight.

Soon the violin was finished, the strings were

stretched, and Vuillaume, hiding a smile, handed the new thing to the nervous inventor.

Savart picked up the bow and drew it across the strings. How they sounded! A bit harshly, but that was only a beginning!

Angular, the shape of a trapezium, and with a straight-sided body instead of the fine, feminine one of a Strad, Savart's violin made quite a stir among acousticians. Its tone was not bad. You would not believe it was coming from so crude a thing. Many of the violins copied from Italian masterpieces sounded worse. The new instrument was even approved by such an authoritative establishment as the French Academy of Sciences.

Little by little, however, the stir about the invention quietened down. The final verdict was given by the performers and not by the scientists. Nobody seemed eager to play the "scientific" violin. The time-tested Strads and Guarneris had a much better tone.

So, Savart's mathematics had failed to catch the subtlety of the violin. Also his instrument looked ugly, more like a coffin than a violin.

Today, very few violinists know this story. The unorthodox instruments of the French physicist can only be seen in museums. In the history of science Savart is better known for his contributions to the theory of electromagnetism.

However, violin-makers and acousticians have great respect for the first investigator of the violin as a resonator. A century and a half ago he tried to unravel what is not fully understood even today. So how can one blame him for his failure?

There was another scientist who took a great interest in the violin. He was Dmitry Chernov of Russia, a metallurgist. He believed that "the manufacture and assembly of the essential parts of these instruments may be likened to the manufacture and assembly of chronometers, microscopes, telescopes and similar precision instruments".

Aware of Savart's failure, Chernov did not attempt to re-style the classical shape of the violin. He used a different method. He bought inferior violins made either at a factory or by some none-too-skilled maker, and studied them thoroughly. Then he took them apart and made what seemed minor changes which would transform the sound beyond recognition. The goal was simple—to correct the mistakes of a "furniture maker", and to turn his excuse of a violin into a perfect resonator capable of picking up and reproducing faithfully the vibrations of the strings. This called for a different approach to different makes and materials.

In 1911 Chernov's violins were put to a crucial test; in the St. Petersburg Conservatoire they were played alternately with violins from Cremona before a panel of leading musicians. The violins were played behind a screen so that the audience could not see which one was being played. Chernov won. Many of his instruments were graded on a par with the Cremona masterpieces.

During the last few decades such contests have become a tradition. Very often the winners would be those who had sought new approaches, investigated sound, read articles on acoustics, and studied the theory of elasticity and the strength of materials. The Soviet school of violin-makers has had excellent results. Its founders, Yevgeny Vitachek and Timofei Podgorny were both scientists and skilled masters and have passed down to their numerous disciples and followers their findings and views.

The German violinist, maker and acoustician Karl Fuhr also made valuable contributions to the art of violin-making. He carried the science of the violin resonator another step further.

The most thrilling pages in the history of the violin, however, were written when violin-makers turned to science for help. In the Soviet Union this happened about a quarter of a century ago.

### WOOD REVEALS ITS SECRETS

The Soviet youth of the thirties will never forget what they were working for in those days. The motto of that time was the inspiring "our own", won with blood. They were working for "our own" industry, "our own" steel, and "our own" coal.

"Down with foreign-made goods!" was their motto. The huge country was squaring its shoulders, and breaking the fetters of economic dependence on the West. And alongside the mammoth projects, quick and sure steps were being taken to tackle another problem—that of setting up a Soviet industry of musical instruments. It was, perhaps, a minor problem but one dear to the human heart.

It had its own enthusiasts and its own difficulties. Its major difficulty was the lack of materials. Not that we did not have enough metal. There was enough brass, and this was the same everywhere. Strange as it may seem, the trouble lay in the wood.

But Russia was rich in wood. And now, of all things, there were no boards for violins and guitars. What a paradox!

Yet that was how things stood. Before the revolution Russian makers of musical instruments bought wood abroad. Because of century-old traditions, eagerly maintained by the owners of "sacred" groves and woods, the bellies of violins and cellos were made from Czech fir, and the backs from Austrian maple. The hallmark of the material was not its quality, but the return address on the parcels for which gold had to be paid.

"It's now time to put an end to this outdated tradition and find our own 'musical' wood." This decision was taken at the Musical Engineering Institute just founded in Leningrad.

The research programme was headed by Professor Nikolai Andreyev, today a Fellow of the Soviet Academy of Sciences and the dean of Soviet acousticians. Before long he came upon an effective method for selecting what physicists call "resonance" wood.

The professor summed up his discovery in very simple terms: The belly should conduct sound waves as quickly as possible to prevent the vibrations colliding and producing unwanted standing waves. These would cause detrimental nodal lines to appear, making the belly swing like a rocker, and pushing the air to and fro instead of breaking it up. So the first requirement of a "resonance" wood was that it should have a high velocity of sound in it.

The next essential was that the swing of the belly should be made as large as possible. Only then would the violin give a good "stir" to the air. For a large swing a light and mobile belly was needed. So, the second requirement of a "resonance" wood was low weight or density.

Finally, there it was, a mathematical formula for a "resonance" wood. The velocity of sound waves was in the numerator and the density of wood in the denominator. The greater this fraction, termed the acoustic constant, the better the wood.

To tell the truth, the acoustic constant was not that simple to derive. It was based on investigations into the structure of wood by crystallographic methods. Later, another Soviet acoustician, Andrei Rimsky-Korsakov (the grandson of the famous composer) extended Andreyev's formula to include one more physical quantity which takes care of the rate of damping of vibrations in wood. Thus, for the first time in the world, a scientific guide was worked out for the selection of "musical" wood.

Scouts were sent to all corners of the country to look for resonance wood. And they found it in many forests, some species as good as and some even better than the foreign ones.

## OFF THE ASSEMBLY LINE

In the meantime, the first factory in the Soviet Union making the violin family of instruments was getting under way in Moscow. It had been designed and organized by another enthusiast, the chief engineer of the musical instruments industry Israel Alender. He was an energetic and sharp-tongued man and had had to fight quite a number of opponents.

"The creative process of the violin-maker cannot be mechanized!" his opponents said.

"It cannot only be mechanized but can also be automated! The manufacture of violins is straightforward wood-working coupled with acoustics," he answered. Matching his deeds to his words, he bought automatic machine-tools for his factory to make violin bellies.

"The violin is the fruit of artistic inspiration! It is a soul embodied in wood," his opponents insisted.

"That's simply idealism! Mysticism! The violin is material plus shape, and nothing more," he retorted.

Material plus shape. The idea was not new. All genuine masters felt that way. But now it had been given a new meaning.

The material had revealed to scientists almost all of its secrets. Andreyev's acoustic constant had given a clue to Stradivarius's remarkable "hunch" in selecting the wood for violins. Indeed, knowledge had now outgrown the intuition of the legendary grand master.

As to shape, things were different. The subtleties of the violin resonator kept evading mathematical treatment. So Alender took the long and painstaking road of trial and error. We should analyze sound so as to get to the physical roots of its beauty, he said. While his factory was turning out cheap but solid violins for the rapidly expanding network of music schools, Alender was laying the groundwork for a research programme with a daring ultimate goal. He hoped to make automatic machines produce violins better in quality than the masterpieces of the ancient Italian makers.

It would be an idle dream to hope that this goal could be achieved overnight. The long succession of failures since Savart's time emphasized how formidable the task was. Yet the research worker had drawn up a plan for many years to come and set down to work, with his sleeves rolled up.

### LEARNING WORDS

Everything had to begin from the beginning, from learning words.

When asked what sort of a violin they wanted, musicians said, "A good violin". That was too vague. The idea needed to be worded more precisely.

The violinists readily explained that a good violin should have a deep and warm tone with a silvery hue. Violins with a clear and noble tone were not bad either, but those with a sandy or nasal voice were no good. They had a rich vocabulary, impressive and imaginative. But none of the words had any bearing on sound.

You may expect sharpness from an axe, colour from a paint, and warmth from a fire-place.

The only thing to do was to try to pick out the acoustical sense from the violinists' lingo. So Alender decided to invite musicians, play different violins to them, ask them to describe the quality of each, and then to analyze the violins scientifically.

A whole panel of musicians was called in. Each was given a questionnaire to fill in giving his opinion of the violins.

The experts were seated before a screen, behind which the violins were played in turn. Everything seemed in order. Before long, however, snags began to appear.

For one thing, the experts conflicted in their judgement. With only the sound of a violin to rely on, their opinions about each instrument were poles apart.

A Conservatoire professor would contemptuously call a violin "twangy", while his no-less competent colleague would give it the complementary epithet "velvety". How could they find out what kind of a violin it really was? Even the opinion of a single expert would sometimes take fancy turns.

Laughingly, Alender recalls a funny story which happened to a well-known musician. His opinion of the "examinees" changed completely overnight. At first, he gave them all a "two" at the most (using the five-point system of marks as of the Russian school) or, more often, a "one", a "one minus", or a "naught". None of them was good enough for him. Even when the noble

Strad was put among the factory-made things it earned an undeserved "two".

One day a deluge of "fours" and "fives" broke loose. Why? It turned out that the expert had been courting a girl. At first she turned him down (the period of "twos" and "ones"), and then she accepted his proposal of marriage (the period of "fours" and "fives").

There were snags everywhere. The experts' mood would change for all sorts of reasons—because of the weather, because of the news in the papers, because of the international situation, because of a recent football game.

The mood of the violinist behind the screen also had to be reckoned with. He knew what sort of a violin he was playing each time. When it came to a Strad, he would feel elated and reverent, and the emotionally sensitive audience would immediately know the difference.

Yet this was the only way to grade the instruments. To disregard the opinions of the experts was to doom the whole undertaking to failure, as had happened to Savart in his time.

The acoustic study of the instruments followed.

### SEVEN KILOMETRES OF WALLPAPER

With Rimsky-Korsakov's assistance, Alender set up a laboratory at his factory. When he came from Leningrad, Rimsky-Korsakov went straight to the room, paced it out, tapped at the walls, thought a little and said it needed more wallpaper.

"How much?" agreed Alender.

Rimsky-Korsakov looked round again, jotted down some figures and said, "Seven kilometres."

"Seven what?" Alender asked, embarrassed.

"Seven kilometres," Rimsky-Korsakov repeated imperturbably. "Your supplies man will have to rob some shop."

They bought a lot of wallpaper—a whole truckload. It was pasted up in an unusual way—across the walls and ceiling, and not from top to bottom. The ridges made closely spaced slots where any sound would be caught in a sort of maze. And that was the goal, so that no reverberations or echoes could interfere with the "surgery" of the violin's tone.

Then a technique was worked out for the analysis of instruments.

The violin to be tested was clamped in a frame. Instead of a violinist playing it, it was bowed mechanically by an endless rosin-rubbed ribbon of horse-hairs. The violin was turned so that each string presented itself to the mechanical bow in turn. The sound was picked up by a microphone to be converted into pulses of electrical current, which were fed into an electron spectrometer for analysis. On its 'scope (the same as a TV screen) the multitude of overtones was broken up into an array of luminous traces. This gave the spectrum of the sound. Its pattern told the investigators the composition of the sound and they could identify which overtones made the sound "sunny", "silvery", "velvety", "hollow", "twanging", or "sandy", whichever poetical and imaginative description was given to it.

Alender invited Boris Yankovsky to work on the sound spectra. Yankovsky was a young acoustician, energetic, tireless, brimming with ideas, but thoughtful and thorough. From a comparison of the experts' opinions and the spectra, he learned to separate out a host of estimates into those which were accidental and those which were objective. Gradually, the instruments came to be graded with increasing accuracy.

That was the beginning of a close alliance between musicians and scientists who were looking for the key to the enigma of the subtlest, most sensitive and most whimsical of all the musical instruments. And this was how a violin laboratory came into being, armed with the latest scientific weapons.

### THE GUITAR COMES FIRST

Yankovsky spent days taking photographs, sorting out and taking to pieces the sound spectra of the violin. By keeping in touch with the music experts he was learning how to predict tone colour from the pattern of the spectrum. Gradually he was able to associate acoustical sense with the vague words of the violinists. Science became increasingly sure in translating these words into its own language, which was dry and terse, but exhaustive and precise, in the form of spectral tables and charts.

The people in the laboratory did not like to hurry and did not jump to any hasty conclusions. The work was carried out deliberately, and there were breaks in it. The longest one was imposed by the war—there were other things to think of. After the war, work was resumed.

And again Alender helped with new electronic gear. Rimsky-Korsakov adapted his acoustical analysis to cover any stringed instrument; instead of a mechanical bow, he fitted a device which would strike the resonator with a small ball. The strings and the sound-box would respond to a blow of the ball as eagerly as to a bow. Indeed, the spectral patterns became better defined, and instead of four spectra (one for each string), one was enough.

The new device came at the right time. After the war, while carrying on his work on the violin, Yankovsky thought it would be a good plan to try out his findings on the guitar, a less aristocratic sister of the violin's and nearly the most popular of all musical instruments.

With the guitar many things were simpler, and work went on smoothly. In 1951, after a series of experiments in the laboratory, the first guitars made to Yankovsky's design saw the light of day.

No one had made such guitars before. Large, with exquisite curves and specially shaped wooden strips on the back, they gave out a magnificent tone, rich, soft and loud. When they learned about the new unusual instruments, guitarists put their names on the waiting list in the shop in Moscow where they were sold. When the new guitar was heard on the radio, Yankovsky won admirers all over the country. He was flooded with enthusiastic letters.

Finally, everything was done. Prototypes and the description of the process were handed over to the factories. The instrument was found to be easy to make by machines on a mass scale. Unfortunately, however, for some unknown reason, the factories never started production. Yankovsky thought better than to push through his brainchild. He went back to the violin. This time he planned not only to study but also to make violins in a scientific way.

### THE LATHE VIES WITH STRADIVARIUS

Problems kept popping up all the time. After they had found out how to arch the belly, they had to devise a way of measuring its elasticity. Then came the load at the various parts of the belly, the flexure and its limits. Then they had to think about the position of the soundpost and the material for the bridge.

Experimental violins would be studded with electronic transducers, the belly would nearly break under heavy loads, and stroboscopes would keep watch on the tuning. And with every month and year, more and more was learned about how to make the violin as a physico-acoustical device.

Lists of "optimum parameters" were drawn up one after another. Yankovsky found that the main mechanical quality that governed the tonal spectrum of the instrument was the elasticity of the belly and back, or the amount they could sag under a load. Later, he determined the amount of sag for different spectra.

The laboratory was now making truly scientific violins. They were made by Konstantin Belyavsky, another enthusiast and Yankovsky's eager assistant. The violins were presented to a panel of musicians who, like physicians deliberating on a diagnosis, evaluated them. And their opinion rose every time.

In 1957, Yankovsky felt he could say "Everything is ready for an automatic copying lathe to make excellent violins."

Yankovsky turned into a machine designer. Together with Belyavsky and others, he made intricate templates. His desk was crowded with books on mechanical engineering and machine-tools. His hands grew hard from work with wrenches and files; his fingers were stained brown by oil. He re-styled and re-arranged the automatic lathe at the factory so that it could execute exact motions like those of the clever fingers of the immortal Italian masters.

At long last, the lathe was set to work by itself. The copying roller ran round a template, and the milling cutters bit into the dry and light wood. Every eight minutes a belly or a back came off the lathe to be gauged and sorted out by precise instruments.

This gauging was a very vital stage in the manufacture of high-quality violins. In addition to the scientific selection of the wood and precise cutting, gauging ensured that every factory-made violin had the same sound spectrum as the classical model. By Yankovsky's technique, this was done quickly and surely.

In the assembly shop the parts were glued together into violins. They looked plain, boasting of neither exquisite varnish nor fancy ornaments. On the face of it, they were just the "cheap lot" at which the connoisseur makes a wry face. But what about their sound?

Yankovsky picked up a violin and, with a frown, drew the bow. Everything seemed to be all right. But it was too early to celebrate. He did not want to be too hasty in his joy, as Savart once was. As is the custom, the experts had to say "aye" first. It was their opinion that counted.

So forty-four violins, still smelling of fresh varnish, were presented to a panel of experts.

### CATCHING A "CARP"

The "carp" is the Strad among the factory-made violins being tested. To "catch the carp" is to get the Strad. Today the procedure has been perfected and everything proceeds as if following a script.

First a "standard" violin is selected, an average piece which all the experts hold in their hands, try with a bow, tap, scratch and feel. Then they agree on its mark, say a "four". Quite a long time is spent discussing its mark, until all of the panel members agree. That is very important.

Then the test proper begins. This is very boring. All day long, the same violinist repeats the same pieces, say Bach's *Chaconne* (for accordatura), the beginning of the first and second movements of Tchaikovsky's violin concerto (for tone colour) and a fragment of Paganini's *Moto perpetuo* (for response to fingering). Each violin takes about five minutes to test and then the "standard" violin is played for two minutes, lest the panel members forget the yardstick with which to make their comparison.

After two hours of patient, painstaking and tiring work during which the panel members try hard to catch the "carp", they sum up their scores.

In the autumn of 1959, the factory-made violins manufactured by the new process won their first victory, which stunned everyone, including Yankovsky. Fourteen out of the forty-four violins had a better score than the "carp"!

For the panel, this was a failure which they took with a heavy heart. It was humiliating not to get a Strad among the "common stock".

But even now it was too early for Yankovsky to rejoice. There had been too many cases when victory had proved accidental. The violin-makers remembered too many disappointments. Besides, the "carp" was, as sceptics insisted, "poor", although made by the Cremona master.

Yankovsky and his staff spent a year improving the scoring system and testing the violins again and again with a host of devices. In the autumn of 1960, they were put through a repeated and more severe test.

The best violinists and musicologists agreed to test them. The "carps" were several unexcelled Italian masterpieces, among them Prince Yusupoff's Strad which had once been bought for a huge sum of money, stolen and hidden like a rare diamond.

This time the panel used the "big scoring scale" of twenty-five points. The experts were attentive as never before.

The final score was this. Two Italian violins (Yusupoff's Strad and a violin by the remarkable master Francesco Ruggieri of the Amati school) scored, respectively, 24.6 and 24 points. The concert violins made by the team of Denis Yarovoi, an outstanding Soviet master and a prize-winner at an international contest at Cremona, had a score nearly as high. One of Yankovsky's experimental violins earned an average of 23.5 points (from two counts), just one point short of Yusupoff's Strad. Some of the other experimental instruments also came off with a high score.

So the panel did catch two "carps". The rest were left in the "pond". Instead, new "fish" of high quality had been discovered. The "scientific" violins had won another convincing victory. Yet, as expected, the experts would not surrender; it was unnatural, there was some flaw in the scoring system.

Why, you cannot dismiss expert opinion.

### ARTIFICIAL AGING

Day after day the factory staff improves the scoring system and tries to refine the violins further. So far they are below the Italian violins in quality. Then there is one more point to think about; the factory-made instruments are given a high grading when played at least seven metres from the panel. Close to, their sound is a bit too harsh and sharp. You can feel the fresh timbre, as a violinist has aptly remarked.

The small team is full of hope. Before them is the same goal that Alender worked for—to make on automatic machines violins which would excel the old Italian instruments without any reservations. New experiments have now been planned to reach this goal. What experiments you may ask?

The time has come to settle an old dispute among musicologists and musicians. Does a violin improve with use and age? Opinions differ. Some insist it does not. A poor violin will remain inferior, no matter how long it is used, they say, and point to the thousands of ordinary instruments for orchestras and students which have surely been played more than any Italian masterpiece but which have remained inferior. Others take a different view. During a performance, they say, a violin is working and its parts interact, and this has an effect on the violin. It is not at all unlikely that a freshly made Strad sounded just like a new factory-made piece. While an inferior instrument may not improve, a good violin will.

Yankovsky hopes to prove, or disprove, this theory through experiment. His plan is to age a successful experimental violin artificially and to watch the changes that occur in its acoustical spectrum. This can be done on a vibrating frame, or by means of a "mechanical bow", with ultrasound, or using radioactivity. He is already working on the idea with the assistance of nuclear physicists. The attack on wood continues.

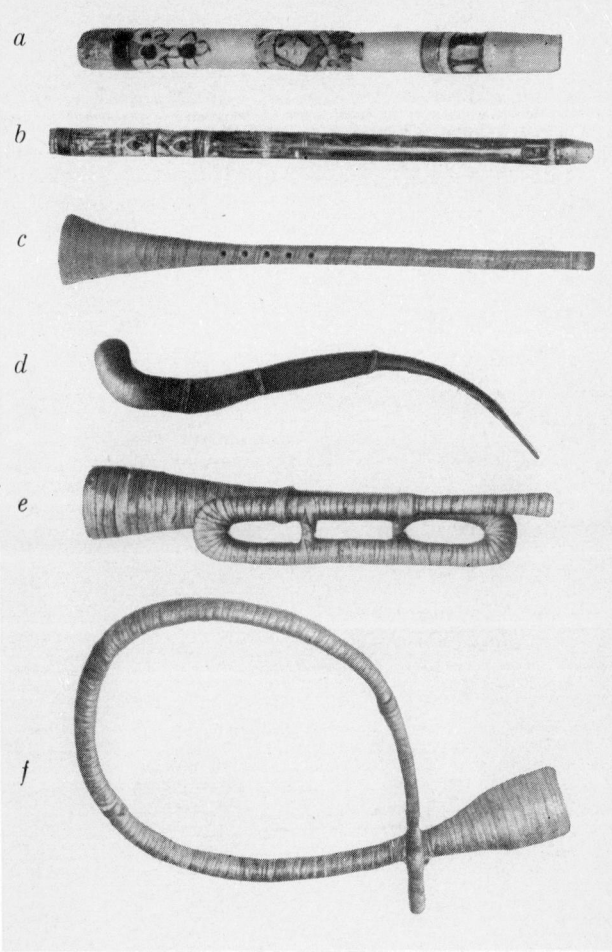

Wind instruments.
a, b—svirels, Russian flageolets; c—a bass horn for a horn-band; d—a shepherd's horn; e, f—trumpets

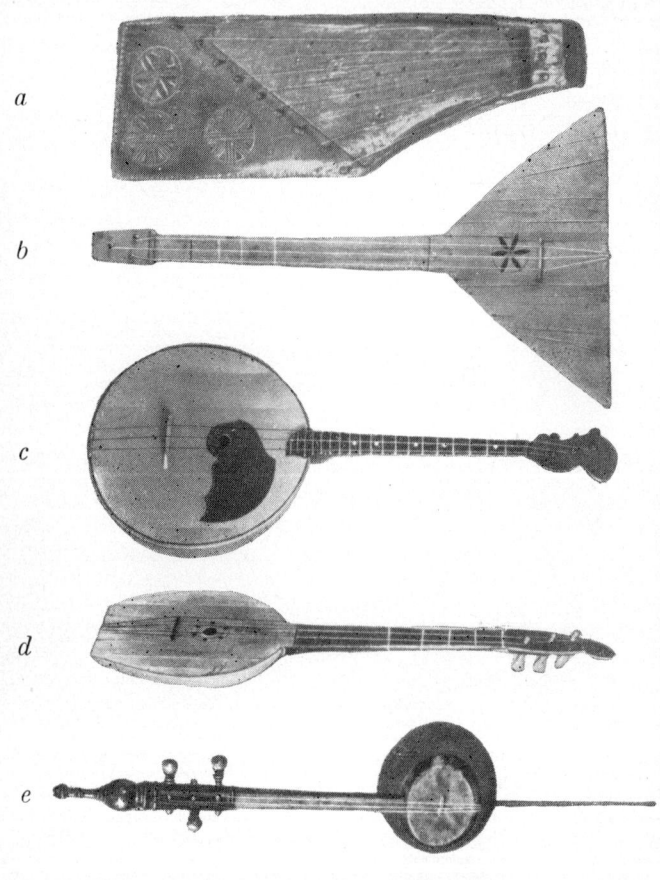

*Stringed instruments.*
*a*—the gouslis, 19th century; *b*—the balalaika; *c, d*—the domras (a reconstruction); *e*—the Uzbek hidzhak

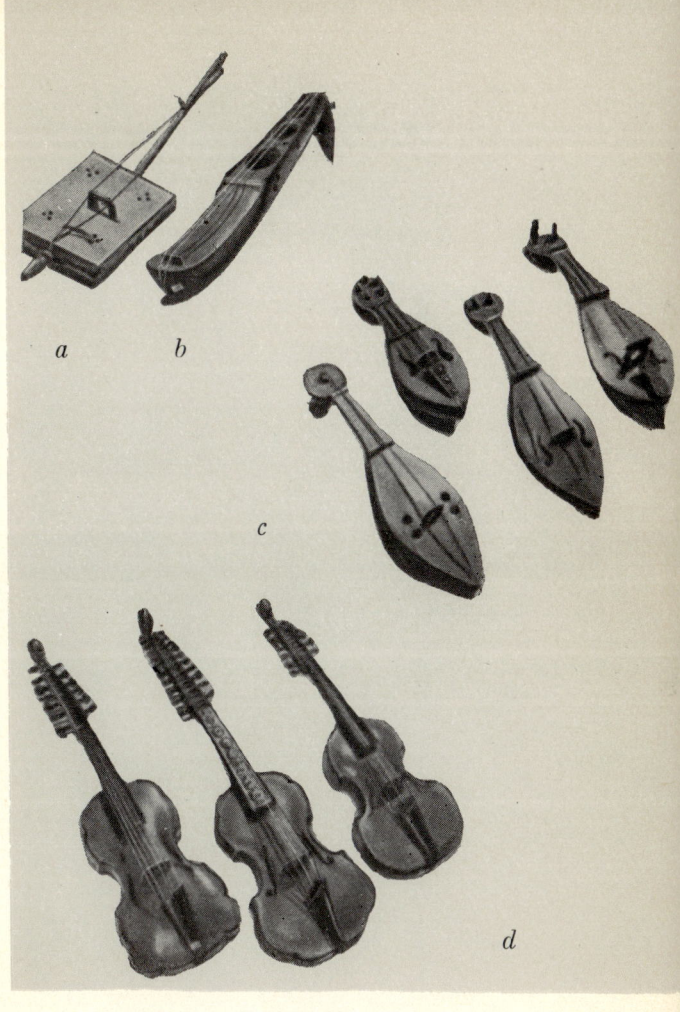

*The violin and its predecessors.*
a—*the Indian ravanstron;* b—*the rebab;* c—*the rebecs;*
d—*the violas*

Forerunners of the piano.
a—the clavichord, 13-14th century; b—the spinet; c—the harpsichord

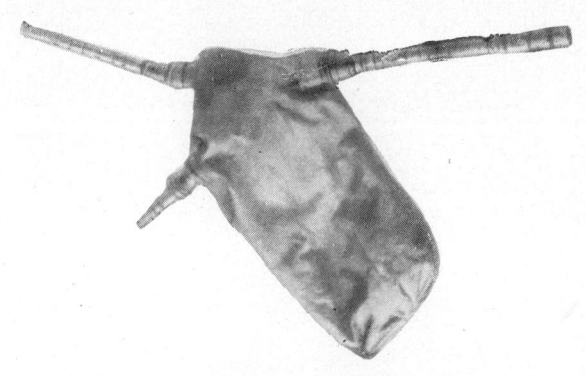

*The chimpoi, a Moldavian bag-pipe*

*The present-day organ*

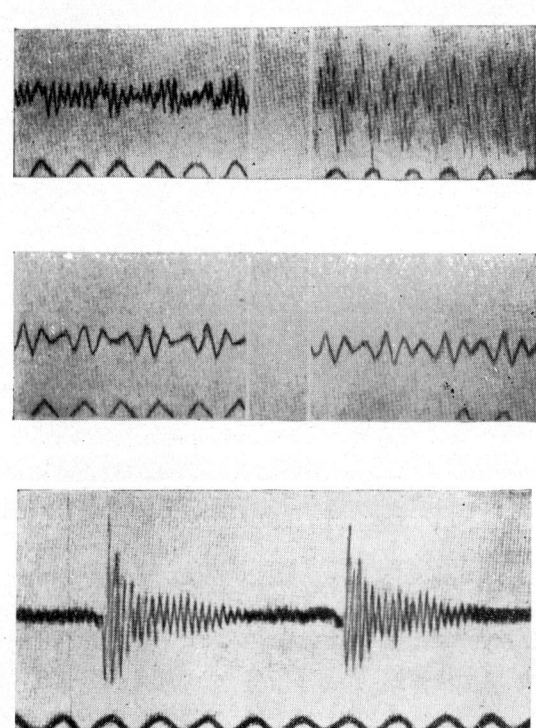

*Oscillograms of a human voice*

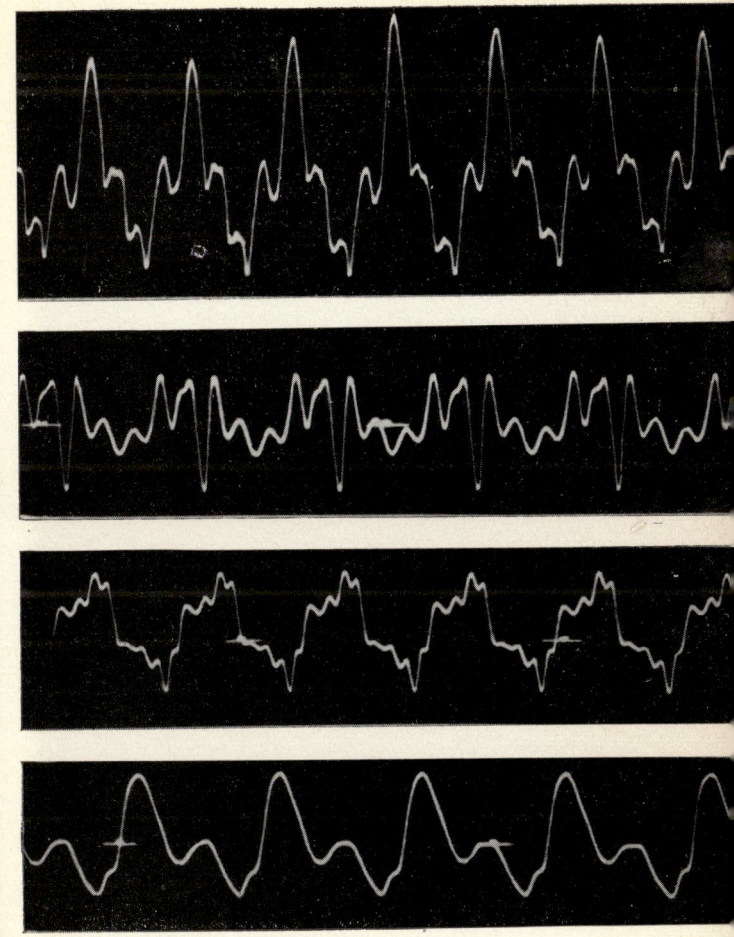

Oscillograms of musical instruments

*The monochord*

*Helmholtz's resonators*

*Berliner's gramophone, 1894*

Much remains to be done. There is even a chance that the material for the violin may be changed. Instead of fir and maple, a special fibrous plastic might be used, light in weight, elastic, strong of unexcelled acoustical properties, exceptionally uniform, free from any knots or knolls, and easy to work. Incidentally, Andreyev did some research in this direction before the war.

The chances are that the day is not far off when superb violins, cellos and guitars will be turned on automatic lathes or simply pressed like cigarette-cases or soap-boxes. Then not only famous virtuosi but every student in a music school and every member of an orchestra will have an instrument which could have enraptured Paganini himself.

An idle dream? No. In our age, it is very likely to happen.

CHAPTER FOUR

\*

# Voice Analysis

What do you think is the basis of all the progress acousticians have made in unravelling the enigma of the violin?

An observant reader will immediately say, "the physical analysis of sound."

Today the art and science of sound analysis have been brought to perfection. The "dissecting" of sound "like a corpse" which Pushkin's Salieri boasted of and the resolution of sound into a spectrum of overtones which Helmholtz accomplished have become the most important tools of musical science.

Devices to convert the voice of trumpets and the strumming of strings into luminous traces on 'scopes are at work in the laboratories of many musical instrument factories. Taking the Soviet Union, they help to improve the piano at the Zarya Factory near Moscow, where Nikolai Dyakonov, a prominent piano expert, carries on his research. They can also be seen at the Lunacharsky Factory in Leningrad which makes guitars, balalaikas, domras and fairly good harps.

In the acoustics laboratory of the Moscow Conservatoire, they analyze the human voice. You can hear a student vocalist say, "They've had my voice for a test-count."

There is nothing strange about it, though. Man's vocal mechanism has much in common with ordinary musical instruments. It has vibrators—elastic tendons vibrating at sound frequencies, and resonators—the cavities of the throat and mouth. A singer's voice is a musical sound as regards both its source and its quality. It can therefore be subjected to acoustical analysis. With the human voice, however, analysis is rather unusual.

### STRETCHING THE VOICE

Perhaps, you can see nothing musical as you enter the laboratory. It smells of rosin (used for soldering and not for violin bows), the technicians are bent over some electrical apparatus and there is a blackboard covered with formulae. This is the same as you can see at a radio factory or in an industrial laboratory.

But, although the laboratory does not look musical, it sounds it. One of the rooms has its walls upholstered with soft fabric. This is where the investigators take their "catch". A thunderous bass gives way to a wooing tenor, and the tenor is replaced by a florid soprano. The singers let the scientists tear their voices to pieces.

Now a young girl whose name may well appear on playbills before long sings the Swan's arioso from *The Tale of Tsar Saltan*. The voice is superb. Dmitry Yurchenko, the laboratory chief, listens attentively. After the arioso, he asks the girl to sing a single, long note. As she sings, the technician turns on a tape-recorder, and the sound is recorded on tape.

"And now listen to what you've sung," says Yurchenko. The technician turns the tape-recorder to play-back.

What happens next is both unexpected and unpleasant to hear. Instead of the girl's ringing voice, a low and wavering sound comes from the speaker. The girl makes a wry face. With a smile, Yurchenko explains:

"We've played a trick on your voice. Now it's stretched, as if it were a rubber cord or a spring. The tape is moving at half the recording speed, and the sound is now halved in frequency so that it is lowered in pitch and extended in duration. Of course you won't be very pleased by it, but we can learn a thing or two about a very important feature of your voice—the *vibrato*."

And what is *vibrato*? Music theorists define it as "a pulsation of pitch, usually accompanied by a synchronous pulsation of loudness and timbre".

The *vibrato* is the most important of the musical ornaments which gives a pleasing flexibility, tenderness and richness of tone to good singing. As physicists have found, the average rate of the *vibrato* of a good singer is 6 to 7 cycles per second. A higher or lower rate of *vibrato* is a sign of poor training or even of disease.

So it is vital to detect an abnormality as early as possible, before it becomes noticeable to the ear. Physicists have devised many methods of doing this, but the simplest is to "stretch" the voice. Then the rate of the *vibrato* can be counted by a stop-watch. Another device counts the rate of *vibrato* without stretching the voice. This is the *vibrato* meter developed by the Conservatoire's laboratory. Voice-trainers can use it, unaided by a technician.

The study of *vibrato*, however, is the simplest example and therefore is not typical of what is done at the laboratory. A good deal of research is devoted to far more subtle and, sometimes, paradoxical qualities of the human voice.

### WHEN THE SINGER IS SILENT

For years Yevgeny Rudakov, a research worker at the Conservatoire laboratory, has been in correspondence with the French scientist Raul Husson, who put forward an intriguing electrophysiological theory of singing. A physiologist and singer himself, Husson refutes the old concepts of the excitation of the vocal cords as the basis of singing.

At one time it was thought that the vocal cords were like the reeds of an accordion, vibrating under the pressure of air. The cords were believed to be stretched and made to vibrate by the air from the lungs. The longer the cords, the lower the voice. The stronger the breath, the louder the sound. Simple, isn't it?

But the human voice is not an accordion. This primitive explanation of the live vibrator failed the test of experiment. The vocal cords of many famous singers, such as Chaliapin and Caruso, have proved to be much smaller than they ought to be according to the old theory. Recently, a young man turned up in Italy with such large vocal cords that, according to the old concepts, his voice should have sounded like a ship's horn. As it happened, he had a fairly feeble tenor.

To cut a long story short, the human voice is far more complicated than an organ pipe. The cords can be set vibrating without the mechanical force of air. As Husson has shown, the human voice is a sort of electrophysiological "speaker". The cords are excited by electric pulses coming to the throat straight from the brain. This action is the basis of the new theory of singing.

The most amazing thing is that even when a singer is not singing, but listening to a piece of music or following the tune in his mind, his cords are vibrating all the same and with the frequency of actual singing. These vibrations can be picked up by electronic instruments. So, you can record what a singer sings in his mind!

We have thus come by a method to test a man's ear for music without making him sing. The examiner sounds a note on the piano and asks an applicant to think about the note. If he "thinks right", the vibrations of his vocal cords, silent but "recordable", will be in exact sympathy with the note.

### SOPRANO OR MEZZO-SOPRANO?

In the life of every singer there is a crucial decision which depends not so much on the singer as on his teacher. This is when a singer's voice is identified for the first time. You see, it is not at all easy to tell a baritone from a tenor or a soprano from a mezzo-soprano when the voice has not yet been trained or refined. There existed no ready-made method of doing this until quite recently. In a dubious case, the examiner would make a guess and choose the method of training accordingly. If he happened to be wrong, his student would waste valuable time or even spoil his voice.

Unfortunately, this still happens now. But guesswork is definitely on the way out thanks to Husson's theory.

In his "electrophysiological" classification, Husson groups all voices on the basis of chronaxy, the excitability of the nerves which control the vocal cords. Chronaxy is measured like this. A transducer is applied to the neck of a singer, and an electronic generator sends out electric pulses through the muscles. At the same time it notes which of the pulses causes the muscle to contract, and displays the result on the dial. A chronaxy of 0.08 identifies a soprano, while a chronaxy of 0.1 points to a mezzo-soprano.

Just think of this; the voice can be identified objectively. The applicants do not have to sing or to utter a single note which is a great convenience to the examiner. Also, no mistake can be made.

So science has devised ingenious ways and means for listening even to silent singers. It displays no less dexterity when it comes to testing the timbre of voices. This is done in the way the resonators of musical instruments are tested.

**DISSECTING THE VOICE**

Another experiment is under way in the Conservatoire laboratory. A student with a strong and rich bass sounds a long note. Its "electric replica" is fed from the microphone into an amplifier and then to an oscilloscope with a screen ruled with coordinate lines. On the screen the voice, or rather the sound wave associated with it, is depicted as a waveform. Voices differing in timbre produce different waveforms. So the waveforms are the labels of timbre.

To make the analysis more precise and less laborious, use is made of what is called a harmonic analyzer. The analyzer has a series of radio filters. When the record of a voice is played back or a singer sings into a microphone, the electrical signal is fed into the filters, and they each "cut out" a particular overtone. At the same time an indicator reads the energy carried by each overtone. On the screen the voice is portrayed as an array of strips. Each strip stands for a particular overtone. The overtones carrying more energy are shown by the longer strips. This is the acoustic (or harmonic-content) spectrogram of the voice. And again, voices differing in timbre produce different spectrograms.

The operation is none too pleasant to the ear; the voice is literally dissected into indescribable squeaks and squeals. You can hardly believe that the sonorous bass of the tall, broad-shouldered singer can contain these high, thin and shrill sounds which seem purely feminine. Yet, this is a fact; they have all been extracted from a male's bass.

#### HOW FAR THE VOICE CAN CARRY

When investigators compared the spectrograms of a great number of professional male singers, they discovered that for a good voice two groups of overtones, or formants, were essential. One is the low formant, with frequencies round about 500 cycles. The other is the high formant lying between 2,400 and 3,200 cycles. The low formant gives the voice its "resonance" or "roundness" or "sonority". The high formant contributes the "ring" or "shimmer". What is more important about any voice, however, is how far it can carry.

The word 'carry' may sound strange in association with the voice. It seems more appropriate to a truck or a crane. Vocalists use the word to describe the ability of a voice to reach a long way.

It may be noted that a voice which carries well is not necessarily a loud voice. Quite the opposite is often the case. A singer may have a small voice, but it can be heard distinctly from a distance. Another singer may have a strong voice which sounds thunderous near by but is hardly audible in a big auditorium.

Today the enigma of the voice's carrying power, which has haunted vocalists for years, has been unravelled by scientists. Working along the lines mapped out by Professor Sergei Rzhevkin, his followers have shown that a voice will carry a long way if it has a well marked high formant. Without it, the voice is dull and colourless; with it, the voice is bright and ringing. A singer with a marked high formant finds it easy to learn good enunciation. You will not have to strain to catch the words as he sings.

Scientists have also explained the physiological factor that makes a voice carry over a distance. As Rudakov has noticed, a singer not only sings but also whistles—with his throat. As in whistling with the lips, the vocal cords produce a high-pitched sound. A good singer should therefore learn how to produce an artistic "whistle" in his throat.

The ear is most sensitive to the frequency of this "throat whistle" or the high formant. Incidentally, the time signals transmitted over the radio are also of high frequency; they can be heard from far away, and they can easily override speech and music.

The fact that the human ear is most sensitive to high-pitched sounds explains why good female voices are more numerous than good male voices. In a female voice, the high formant is not so important because sopranos and mezzo-sopranos are rich in the higher tones without it. In a male voice, on the other hand, it is essential.

### BEAUTY BY THE MEASURE

Physicists say that a voice-trainer should seek to develop the high formant in his students. Fine, say voice-trainers. But how can this advice be put into practice? How can one keep tabs on the high formant while a student is singing an aria or exercises? It is hardly practical to analyze a student's voice to determine the overtones each time, and the ear cannot detect minute changes in the frequency spectrum of a voice from session to session.

Again, physicists have come to the rescue. Rudakov has worked out a method of reducing the quality of a voice to the readings on electronic instruments. His colleague Schwarz has devised a timbre indicator. As a singer sings, the instrument keeps constant watch on the quality of his voice. Its readings give the carry factor—a measure of the voice's beauty, if you like.

"Just imagine—beauty by the measure!" you may say. Perhaps it is an exaggeration. What is measured is not the beauty but some of its components inseparable from other properties of the voice.

One way or the other, the timbre indicator is a good aid to the voice-trainer. Imagine that a student comes upon a way of maintaining a pleasant timbre at a lesson. The timbre indicator gives a carry factor of 20. The trainer draws the student's attention to the fact and tells him to carry on in the same way at the next lesson. With the indicator to help, the student finds it easy to do this.

A reader with an ironical turn of mind may say, "It looks as if in the long run instruments are going to replace human beings for examining student vocalists. It may so happen that your timbre indicators will oust the concert-goers!"

Joking apart, instruments stand in good stead in exams at the Moscow Conservatoire, though only as part of scientific studies. In the future they will surely become reliable study aids for student vocalists.

### THE MYSTERY OF THE VOICE

Analysis of the tone of the violin opened up a way to making violins of high quality. Likewise, when it has fully solved the riddle of the human voice, acoustics will be able to help singers to make fuller use of what nature has given them. Perhaps even nature herself may be surpassed. Physicists, physiologists and voice-trainers may learn how to turn anyone into a good singer, not just a few prodigies. Many scientists consider that there is nothing to stand in the way of this goal. Before it can be realized, however, there is much to be investigated, tested and understood.

Today there are still many problems concerning the acoustics of the singing voice. Take, for example, the four-octave voice of Ima Soumak who feels quite at home in all the traditional female compasses from the contralto to the colorature soprano. The amazing Peruvian can even sing male baritone and bass parts, although they sound unusually feminine. Equally amazing is her ability to change her timbre and pitch at will and to produce a "double sound", as if two singers are performing and not one. This surely is proof of the inexhaustible potentialities of the human voice, still unexplained and showing themselves very seldom, almost by chance. There is plenty for singers, scientists and voice-trainers to think about.

Ima Soumak is not alone. Other singers of lesser fame can also produce the double sound. Apparently, it is the result of a special way of timbre control. It is not unlikely that scientific research into this effect will place it within the reach of many a singer.

The human voice has the greatest flexibility of all musical instruments. At the same time, it is extremely complex. It seems strange that the shrill and thin tones of the high formant of the baritone and the bass cannot be heard separately. Why is it that they merge together to give a rich, low sound?

The acoustic spectrograms recorded at the Conservatoire's laboratory seem hopelessly baffling. Judge for yourself. In the spectrograms of a bass, the fundamental tone accounts for only a negligible fraction of the total energy. Sometimes there is no fundamental tone to be seen at all, although we can hear it distinctly. It turns out that the singer builds up the fundamental tone out of thin higher overtones. It is like a female choir singing Konchak's roaring part in *Prince Igor*. A hundred tall "laths" on the spectrogram go to make a single short "log". An amazing thing!

As you will learn from the next chapter, acoustics has already explained it. The answer was found by relating the human voice to the human hearing mechanism which is responsible for the perception of music. Indeed, you cannot possibly have a proper understanding of the physics of music without a knowledge of the physics of hearing.

CHAPTER FIVE

*

## Tones Created by the Ear

Some time ago a science-fiction play featuring Martians, robots and other mysterious characters was being rehearsed at a radio studio. The actors were trying hard to make their voices sound "unearthly". But in vain. The voices just did not sound "inhuman".

"Tell your robots to shout into the piano with the damper pedal down," the shrewd sound engineer told the stage director. The director did as he was told, and the trick worked—the piano strings with the dampers off responded to the human voice and added a metallic ring to it.

Today radio directors producing plays about space flights and distant worlds often use this trick. You can try shouting into a piano yourself. The piano will echo with fairly distinct a's, e's, o's and u's.

A hundred years ago Helmholtz spent quite a lot of time shouting into his piano. Very likely this prompted him to analyze musical sound. For the piano is a typical analyzer; the strings sound in sympathy only with corresponding tones in the human voice. Perhaps it was the piano that suggested to him his intriguing ideas about the human hearing mechanism.

### THE PIANO IN THE EAR

Although educated as a physician, Helmholtz was equally good as a physicist or a physiologist. He would forget the time, while studying the excised hearing organs of man and animals. Before him was an alluring goal—to learn what made the ear work.

It was no easy task. At first, the scientist found himself on a sidetrack. Reluctantly, Helmholtz abandoned his original 'resonance theory of hearing'. But he did not lose heart, and finally his persistance won.

In the inner ear he was looking for, and found, a tiny semblance of the piano with twenty thousand "strings", nerve terminals in the form of small hairs differing in length. A "string" for each frequency of the sound wave! This live resonator-analyzer, called the basilar membrane, is hidden in the cochlea, a bony spiral tube of two and three-quarter turns, filled with fluid.

As Helmholtz saw it, the sound wave travels through the fluid of the cochlea across the "strings", and the hair cells respond at once by resonating and exciting the nerve fibres running to the brain.

Later, scientists changed their ideas somewhat about the hearing mechanism. Apparently, not only the basilar membrane but also the fluid in the cochlea is capable of resonance. This tube, the shape of a snail shell, acts like the resonator of a wind instrument. The fluid filling it is traversed by long and short waves. The waves close into arcs and strike different places on the basilar membrane, much as a pianist's fingers work the keys.

True, this is only a very rough sketch of the actual process. The physiology of hearing is still being explored. It is very complex, involving, as it does, biopotentials, mechanochemistry, electronics and cybernetics. Some of its peculiarities are just as complex, and deserve special mention.

**GHOST SOUNDS**

In the 18th century the Paduan violinist Giuseppe Tartini came across something very intriguing. One day, while getting ready for a performance, he was working on double sounds by bowing two strings at a time. His ear was alert listening to his violin. When the two strings were bowed strongly, he could hear what he later called *terzi suoni* (third sounds), lower in pitch than the two actually sounded. It gave the impression that there was a third string stretched loosely between the other two.

Later the third sound was also noticed by the German organist Sorge. Soon this tone, called a 'combination' tone because it is the result of the simultaneous sounding of two other tones, came to be heard by many musicians. Physicists learned that its frequency was the difference between those of the two "parent" tones, and so the "illegitimate child" was called a 'difference' tone. But how did it come about?

Helmholtz again was the first to give a correct answer. As it turned out, the difference tones are "ghosts". Musical instruments do not produce them; they are created by the healthy ear itself.

However strange it may seem, when we are listening to music, we "embellish" it against our will. The ear and the brain are not only sound analyzers, they are also "musical instruments". Any concert-goer takes part in the orchestra or choir unawares. And this subconscious "creativity" is fairly extensive.

Tartini's "ghosts" are only part of the extras our ear adds to any piece of music we hear. There are also less prominent 'summation' combination tones. Their frequency is the sum of the frequencies of the "parent" tones. They were discovered by Helmholtz. Later scientists added to them 'aural harmonics' with which the ear brightens up sufficiently strong pure single tones. All of these "daughter" sounds may form pairs to produce further "descendants" whose pitch and loudness can be predicted by mathematical analysis.

As Leibniz, the outstanding German mathematician, philosopher and discoverer of differential calculus, remarked, "Music is the soul's unconscious exercise in arithmetic." He is more right than he thought. The brain and the ear are busy "doing arithmetic" all the time, subtracting, adding and multiplying sound frequencies. Even a simple sound, if it is strong enough, may turn into an acoustical rainbow in the listener's mind. It is this rainbow which, in the final analysis, gives any sound its quality.

### LITTLE RED RIDING HOOD AND THE TELEPHONE

Nature does not tolerate excesses. Everything must have a cause and a purpose. Why is it then that the ear creates tones which are not sounded? Why is it that the already complex mixture of overtones is complicated still further?

The answer is simple. In this way man's perception of music is greatly enriched, and is made more flexible and refined. As you strike, or pluck or bow a string, your ear picks up its overtones and sets to work combining them. This is where Tartini's "ghosts" come in. Each pair of tones produces a difference tone. Suppose the fundamental tone is of frequency 100. Then its overtones are of frequencies 200, 300, 400, 500, etc. Any pair of adjacent overtones will produce a difference tone of frequency 100, or the same as the fundamental tone. As a result, the fundamental tone is fortified many times. The difference tone due to two overtones one harmonic apart builds up the first overtone. The difference tone due to two overtones two harmonics apart adds strength to the second overtone, and so on. The ear thus works like a diligent student studying a text-book—it stresses the main thing. The sound becomes steady and well-defined. The ear picks it up unmistakably, even though it may be distorted a good deal. Indeed, the ear has the remarkable faculty of restoring distorted tones.

Supposing we cut the fundamental tone out of a string's sound. The ear will easily cope with such gross abuse. The ear will reconstruct the main tone out of the harmonics as a difference tone. This remarkable "reparative surgery" has been tested in a multitude of experiments. It resembles the breaking of a code, the restoration of a painting discoloured by time, or the much-publicized reconstruction of a face from a skull.

However hard Gray Wolf in the fairy-tale might try to get rid of his deep fundamental tone, the combination tones would immediately betray his blood-thirsty voice to Little Red Riding Hood.

Or take the telephone. For the sake of simplicity and economy it is designed so that very little of the main tones of a conversation are transmitted. Yet the ear restores them faithfully. The speech remains fairly intelligible.

Last but not least, combination tones give the key to the baffling spectrum of the male bass you read about in the previous chapter. A singer's voice may contain very little of the main tone, but the ear will build it up out of the harmonics. Although this is a harder way of "cooking" tones than by using a separate "string" for each of them, the economy is obvious. You can get tones of low pitch without huge vocal cords or large resonators. Nor is much force required to set heavy vibrators in motion. Sound information is thus transmitted with the least expense of energy. Nature has proved a skilled "communications engineer".

### THE WOOD FOR THE TREES

In an orchestra with a dozen violins there are usually two or three double basses and a few cellos. Yet they can be distinctly heard over the violins. Why?

This is because the tones of an orchestra are like a grove of trees on a hill-side. At the foot of the musical range the tallest trees of overtones grow from the low-pitched tones of the double basses and cellos. They span the whole range. Their tops, although unheard by themselves, screen the shorter bushes growing out of the high-pitched tones of the violins and flutes. If it were not for the greater sensitivity of the ear to the higher pitch, we should not hear the violins against the background of the cellos.

Then there are aural harmonics, those ghost sounds. They help the ear to catch pure tones deprived of higher harmonics of their own. The ear is like fertile soil, and the pure tones are like seeds. A pure tone in the ear shoots up like a sapling into a sound tree with branches of aural harmonics. And brightened-up tones are much easier to recognize. For trees differ between themselves more than seeds.

An acoustics engineer with a good knowledge of all these facts can easily calculate the optimum set-up of an orchestra for any piece of music. Incidentally, mathematical orchestration could also give good service to composers and conductors. As often as not, intuition fails. Tchaikovsky is known to have rejected his own opera *Vakula the Smith* because of poor orchestration, because one "could not see the wood for the trees".

So there is an orchestra in the ear, an orchestra in the sound of each instrument, and an orchestra on the stage. As soon as we know the set-up of the first, we can get a better idea of how to arrange the second and the third. The three, as you can see, are closely related. Even the position of the instruments on the stage is governed by the mechanism of hearing. We deliberately put the high-pitched violins in front of the low-pitched double basses. Counter to Krylov's fable, the musicians must know where to sit.

Sound and hearing make up a strong and inseparable alliance which serves as the foundation for musical acoustics and, indeed, for music as a whole.

Since hearing is inseparable from the brain, and the brain from the whole organism, music has a very important physiological part to play. Physicians have long since learned that music can help or interfere with work, cause a sensation of pain or relieve it. Some dentists give their patients headphones so that they can listen to tape-recorded music while their teeth are being filled. They endure the boring and cleaning better while listening to music than in silence. There is a volume control built into the arm-rest of the chair. As the pain increases, the patient squeezes the arm-rest, the music is played louder, and the pain is then felt less. So music can mask pain.

Much could be said about the growing alliance between music and medicine. But that would lead us too far from our subject. So let us get back to the alliance between music and hearing.

### HARMONY AND DISCORD

When there is nobody around, strike the keyboard of a piano with your fist. It will produce a chord, unpleasant and grating. Now strike any three white keys spaced one white key apart. Can you tell the difference?

Since olden times musicians have been trying to find pleasant combinations of sounds. Thousands of books have been written on the subject, and a host of rules have been devised. Before Helmholtz, however, nobody had tried to trace harmony, or pleasant chords, to physical and physiological roots.

We will not go too far into his theory. It is full of mathematics, 'roughness' charts and other technicalities. The main thing is that the chords most agreeable to the ear are those which use notes separated by simple natural intervals. Every fundamental tone heard in nature is accompanied by its second harmonic (the octave), its third harmonic (the twelfth), and so on. This is why the combination of overtones built up by the ear out of a single tone gives pleasure to the brain. If we construct a similar combination artificially it will also sound agreeable.

So two tones sound well together when the ratio of their frequencies is expressed by the small whole numbers 1, 2, 3, 4. The smaller the numbers, the better the consonance. For the octave the ratio is 2:1, for the fifth (the interval between the octave and the twelfth) it is 3:2.

When he looked through old scores, Helmholtz found that in the past, when chords were just beginning to come into use, European music kept to this fairly simple rule. Giovanni da Palestrina, an Italian composer of the 16th century, wrote his music as if he could have seen Helmholtz's charts and tables of overtones.

Later, composers began to depart from the natural intervals. This is not difficult to explain. Though sweet, chocolate will pall if you have too much of it. Sometimes, a harsh dissonance may prove more agreeable than the most perfect concord.

Every man has his share of sorrow, wrath or tragedy during his life-time. It may well be that musical art deliberately departs from natural harmony so as to render such feelings.

The chances are that the first such departure was the invention of the minor scale (or 'mode') which gives a doleful colour to music. The effect of the minor scale is due to a simple device. Instead of the major (or greater) third consisting of two tones it uses the minor (or lesser) third consisting of one and a half tones. Though small, this difference completely changes the quality of music,—so sensitive is the ear.

European music was slow to accept the minor mode. The unsophisticated ear of the medieval composers heard unnatural roughness in it. Bach himself preferred the gay major mode. Even when he happened to write in the minor scale, he would wind up with a happy major ending. Today, the major and the minor scales are equals. Anthems, marches, festive compositions and playful pieces are written in the major mode. Lyrical, pensive, melancholy, dramatic or sorrowful music is written in the minor scale.

It should be added, however, that this is an arbitrary and approximate classification. There are exquisite marches in the minor scale, and sparkling, playful tunes with a colour of the minor key. The psychology of musical perception is too involved to be squeezed into the simplified major-minor scheme.

The minor scale itself is but one of the many adjustments musicians have made in the mathematical order of tonal sequences. In different nations at different times there have been quite a number of other "departures" from the acoustico-mathematical regimentation of music. Over the centuries a great many such departures, or adjustments, have accumulated. Every nation has used them to develop its own principles and techniques of musical composition— all that is termed a scale, mode, or key. Whatever the name, the goal is the unity of tone.

**UNITY OF TONE**

When we hear a harsh discord, our first thought is that the unrelated tones have been put together haphazardly.

That is true. For unrelated tones are not music. Music involves tones which are related to each other in a recognizable manner.

This can be done in many ways. The same tones are put together differently in Russian, Chinese or Hindu music, especially as far as the intervals between the tones are concerned. Some of them, though, seem to be universal. These are the octave, the fifth and, to a lesser degree, the fourth which is the difference between the octave and the fifth. They are the bedrock of natural harmony. Inside the octave, however, ancient Chinese music had only five notes (the pentatonic scale). European music prefers seven in the diatonic scale and twelve in the chromatic scale.

The history of music has known a great variety of modes and scales, some very common and others not so common. Thus *The Siskin Bird*, a favourite song among Russian children, is in what the Greeks called the Lydian mode (in the 16th century Glarean wrongly called it the Ionian mode), which has survived as our major scale or key. The Russian songs *The Meadow* and *Oh, My Mist* are written in a beautiful, but rather fanciful variable mode common to many Russian folk songs and almost non-existent in Western music.

There are some modes, very involved and peculiar, which sound strange to the European ear, such as those of India and other Oriental countries.

Yet, for all the diversity of musical relationships and national colour, all scales, modes and keys have one thing in common, which also finds its explanation in the laws of sound and hearing. This is tonality, or attaching unique importance to one note.

In any mode, there are stable and unstable notes. The stable note occurs at the end of a melody. Most often, this is the tonic or key note, the first note of a mode. At least, this is so among the majority of civilized races at the present time.

In a musical phrase, the tonic is stressed much as the fundamental tone is stressed among its harmonics by the ear. If the music stops on an unstable note, we refuse to accept the ending place as final. Like a sledge on an icy hill, the music tends to move on, towards its final destination. Just try and sing any song without its final note, and you will see the point at once. The same is true of the accompanying chords. The final chord sounds like the full stop at the end of a verse, while the intermediate chords are more of a comma or a semicolon—they suggest a continuation.

The structure and laws of scales, modes and keys make up the cornerstone of all musical art and science. A great many leading scientists and composers have devoted a good proportion of their time to them. This is not hard to understand. A proper understanding of them gives deep insight into the innermost sources of the musical art of all humanity.

Inseparable from them is the problem of tuning, a matter of failure or success to every musician.

CHAPTER SIX

\*

# The History of Tuning

Imagine yourself as an ancient harpist. You have just made your harp and stretched strings on it, and you are now going to tune the instrument. It must be tuned so that you can play your favourite song or vamp to it at least. But you have more than one song and so you want your harp to be tuned for each of them.

So you tighten the strings in various ways, adding more if necessary, fixing the vital tones, and sacrificing those which seem unimportant. Finally you find what you think is a good tuning. What sort of tuning is it? At best, it should give the musical intervals of the modes used in your country. You have not the slightest idea about the theory of modes and tonal relationships, but your taste and ear lead you inevitably to them.

At last everything is done. The strings of your harp are tuned to the ascending tones of one or two popular modes. For the time being you are satisfied. You find it easy to play your repertoire, and your listeners applaud. Unexpectedly, one of your audience asks you to play a song a bit higher, so that he can sing it more comfortably. Without re-tuning your harp, you try to start from a string higher in pitch—and fail. The intervals between the strings are not equal. As soon as you have shifted the key note, the remaining notes have fallen out of key. To re-tune the strings would take you too much time and, burning with shame, you say the humiliating "I can't".

Another time you fail in an encounter with a foreign guest. You like the tunes he has brought with him, but you just cannot play them, whichever string you start with. Other, unfamiliar scales and modes are used overseas. The intervals in them are different from those in your country. So, again, you have to re-tune your harp.

This time it is more than enough for you. You set to work thinking up a universal tuning, equally good for any scale and for playing from any note. You add more strings and sweat over the hardest problem of musical art. You will not solve it, for it will be left for whole generations of musicians and music theorists to tackle in the centuries to come.

### PYTHAGORAS COMES TO HELP

Today, tuning is no longer a problem. The solution to it is embodied in any keyboard instrument.

Here is the keyboard of a grand piano. It has eighty-eight keys, or eighty-eight notes differing in pitch. This is a modest number if you recall that the musical range extends from 20 to 3,000 cycles per second. But the eighty-eight keys are enough for the pianist to play any composition, however complex it may be. Indeed, he can play any music—Russian, Scottish or Chinese, starting from any note.

How is this accomplished? What is the rule by which the musical scale has been divided into fixed intervals without which the universal tuning and musical notation would have been impossible?

The musical scale is not a measuring scale. You cannot just divide it into, say, a hundred arbitrary units of pitch like you can divide the metre into centimetres. Chosen at will, they would not give a unity of notes. A piano tuned to such a scale would produce harsh discords. Obviously, there is some physical law behind the tuning of the piano.

You surely know that the piano keys are arranged in regular groups of twelve keys each—seven white ones and five raised black ones. There are seven groups of keys in all, each with a compass of an octave.

The octave as a musical interval must have been discovered very early in man's history. The early Greeks seem to have used no other concord in their music. It is the simplest and most perfect consonance of all. Any well-tuned instrument must have it, so that any note can be reproduced an octave up or down. Such is the rule of the ear.

But why are there twelve intervals to the octave, no more and no less?

A dozen notes to the octave is a very clever discovery made by old-time musicians through trial and error. With twelve notes, a melody can be readily played in any mode and started from any key note. The road to this discovery was long and thorny. And the ball was set rolling, as far as we know, by Pythagoras who was the first to standardize the musical scale in terms of mathematics.

Pythagoras believed numbers were the ultimate explanation of all things, including music, especially pleasant tones. He found that simple musical intervals were given by the notes produced by the two segments of a stretched string if the point of division gave segments whose lengths were in a single numerical ratio. He knew that the octave was produced by two segments of a string whose lengths are in the ratio 2:1, and the fifth by two segments whose lengths are in the ratio 3:2. He took a stretched string tuned to the lowest note in use at that time, clamped it at the middle, and sounded one half of the string. The note produced was an octave above that of the open string. Then he clamped the half at its middle and sounded a note which was again an octave up from the previous note. He continued doing this until he had obtained a total of seven octaves within the audible range.

Then he clamped the same string a third of the way from one end and plucked the remaining two-thirds. The interval between the notes produced by the two-thirds and the full length of the string was the fifth, also a familiar pleasant interval. Working this way, he obtained a second fifth, a third fifth, and so on until he got twelve fifths in all. The end of the last (twelfth) fifth came nearly at the end of the last (seventh) octave.

From this relation Pythagoras and his followers devised a complete chromatic scale. Based entirely on the octave and the fifth, it is known as the Pythagorean scale.

### THE COMMA AND THE WOLVES

The Pythagorean scale, however, suffered from many drawbacks. The main trouble was that seven octaves are not exactly equal to twelve fifths. In fact, twelve fifths are greater than seven octaves by what is known as the comma of Pythagoras. As a result, the Pythagorean octave was made up of five tones and two semitones, and not equal tones throughout. So the Pythagorean tuning in fifths was all but perfect.

This was unimportant as long as two notes were not heard together. The rise of harmony, however, changed the situation, especially for keyboard instruments.

Another, somewhat different scale was the natural or true scale. With this was associated a special form of tuning—just intonation. It grew out of a theoretical scale suggested by the Greek musician Aristoxenus and later modified by Zarlino, Maître de Chapelle at St. Mark's, Venice, about 1560. It is so called because the most important of its notes form natural or true intervals with the key note. More important still, these intervals form concords when sounded together.

Unfortunately, justly intoned music gave a sense of monotony. This was because the other notes, not forming natural or true intervals with the key note, denied the composer and performer of keyboard instruments any change of key. If they were to be free to use all keys, they would require eighteen notes to the octave. With the human voice, stringed instruments and many wind instruments there is no limit set to the number of notes that can be used. With the piano and the organ it is a very different matter. Each note requires a separate lever or key, and the mechanical difficulties in design become formidable.

Many attempts have been made to minimize the bad effects of the Pythagorean comma and the comma of Didymus in Zarlino's scale. One of them was mean-tone temperament* which came into being in the 16th century. In its final form, some of the fifths were so flattened, or diminished, that a perfect major third was made out of an unpleasant interval. With the mean-tone system the octave came by twelve notes, or as many as we have today. Indeed, our modern musical notation is based on it.

Unfortunately, along with the improvements, an interval was allowed to creep in, known as the *quinte-de-loup*, or 'wolf fifth'. This howling tone turned out to be very nasty. To keep it out

---

* Temperament is a compromize by which true intonation is sacrificed in order to secure freedom of key modulation for keyboard instruments.

of the music, composers had to choose their key carefully. Organs were sometimes built with additional keys to take care of the "wolf".

Of course, there are always two sides to a story, and there was a humorous side to the "wolf-tone". As the story goes, the composer Jean Philippe Rameau, who was not particularly willing to take up the position of a church organist, skilfully drew "wolves" from his organ. This scared away the clergy who had been too insistent with their offer.

As time passed, others tried to improve upon the musical scale and tuning, among them the astronomer Kepler, and the mathematician Euler. Success, however, was due to Andreas Werckmeister, an organist in Northern Germany. In his *Musical Temperament* published in 1691, he came out with a solution which looks ordinary today.

Werckmeister's plan was simplicity itself. He distributed the comma of Pythagoras equally over the twelve fifths which make up the seven octaves. As the comma is about a quarter of a semitone this involved flattening, or diminishing, each fifth by about a forty-eighth of a semitone. Now the twelve fifths did equal the seven octaves, and the tuning in fifths was free from accumulating inaccuracies. This put an end to the comma and the wolves.

In the new system, the octave was divided into twelve equal divisions. Each division was a tempered semitone, a sort of musical "centimetre". But unlike the ordinary centimetre chosen arbitrarily, the tempered semitone was made to meet the requirements of acoustics and the human ear.

So, made up of tempered semitones, the twelve-interval equal-temperament scale came into being. Today, it is in universal use for keyed instruments in European music.

So you see, it was not an easy job to create it. And its adoption was also slow.

### BACH VERSUS HANDEL

Bach and Handel are the first-order personalities in Europe's music. They were born in the same year. Both were organists and composers. The works of both have survived as the foundation of European classical music. They respected each other although they never met. Yet, there was one point over which they disagreed. That was equal temperament.

Handel did not accept the novelty. He was the sort of musician who ridiculed any departure from the mean-tone system for which he wrote. Nor did the banishing of wolves win him over. Instead, Handel had an organ made with additional keys to "clean up" the inevitable false fifths and thirds. In fact, most of the organists and composers of that time thought the same way.

Bach was the first leading musician to adopt equal temperament. Not only were his own clavichord and harpsichord tuned to it, but also he wrote the well-known *Forty-eight Preludes and Fugues for the Well-tempered Clavier*. With his "Forty-eight" he proved that equal temperament enabled compositions in all keys to be played without wolves or any other disagreeable discords. Yet even he was unable to convert the organ-builders of his time to the new system. Nor did his son, who supported the change, make rapid headway.

For all the resistance, history has proved Bach right. Many musicians, among them Beethoven, Mozart, Chopin, Liszt, Tchaikovsky, Musorgsky, Borodin and Rimsky-Korsakov, have further perfected the system. Musical art owes some of its best creations to equal temperament.

#### FROM GOOD TO BETTER

Today nobody questions the merits of equal temperament. It is admirably simple and offers a lavish choice of keys to play in. It has served us well for centuries and will continue to do so.

Yet, some of the Handel-Bach controversy of the past has remained. Today we wonder whether the question of the musical scale has been finally resolved by Werckmeister's equal temperament, or whether the subdivision will continue? Is it reasonable to chain the orchestra to the eighty-eight keys of the piano for ever? Will the twelve-interval scale remain adequate for the music of the future?

Opinions differ. Some of the latter-day musicologists believe that equal temperament cannot be improved. Their opponents, ignoring the proverb of 'letting well alone', insist that the present twelve-note scale must not be allowed to limit the progress of musical art.

The former say the human ear is not sensitive enough to notice the small difference between natural and tempered intervals, and the indisputable dissonances of equal temperament do not distress us. Anyway, a piano or organ in which every interval can be made perfect would have many more than eighty-eight keys. It would be a monster difficult both to build and to play.

Their opponents are aware of the mechanical difficulties involved. Yet they believe the game is worth the candle. Even now the human ear prefers natural, freely chosen intervals and concords, they say.

Indeed, to a great many good violinists the fifths of the piano and organ sound 'too flat'. When unaccompanied, instead of 'flattened fifths' they use perfect intervals, or even slightly "sharpened" intervals, especially if the music is dynamic and the notes change in rapid succession. The audience likes it, and there is no limit set to the intervals that can be used by a violin free from keys or levers. If a piano joins in, a harsh discord may be heard.

Both composers and performers today are careful enough to avoid clashes between true and tempered intonation. But we may query whether it is reasonable to avoid true intervals which are so beautiful.

Many outstanding musicians and musical theorists have sought concords and intervals beyond the reach of the piano. Our old acquaintance Helmholtz was dissatisfied with the piano, saying that its "every note sounds false and disturbing". In fact, he had a harmonium tuned in true intervals and fitted a multitude of additional keys. Chaliapin liked to sing Volga folk songs in perfect natural intervals, unaccompanied. After a stay in the countryside, Tchaikovsky would feel keenly the defects of tempered music, including his own. The most brilliant proponent of extending the musical scale was, according to some musicologists, the famous Russian composer Alexander Scriabin.

### BETWEEN THE KEYS

If you haven't done so already you ought to hear Scriabin's symphonies, *Poem of Ecstasy* and *Prometheus*. The elements are grasped and tamed by the genius of the composer. It is exquisite music, although not so simple as that of the old masters.

The composer, though, was not always happy about his works. Some of his chords just would not "fit" into the keyboard of the piano. He would compensate for the missing sound by using a trill or shake, the rapid alternation of two notes, one a bit above and the other a bit below the one required. The listener would hear something very near the missing sound.

Near the end of his life Scriabin gave especial thought to overcoming the limitations of the twelve-interval scale. Like Handel and Helmholtz before him, he experimented with additional keys on the keyboard of the piano. He did not live to see the results. Later, when pianos with an extended keyboard were made, they proved too complicated and difficult to play.

During the fifty years since his death, Scriabin's works have stood the rigorous test of time. Today, they are highly valued. Many a good musician appreciates his striving for pure concords and perfect intervals which the tempered scale cannot give. When working on Scriabin's compositions, the well-known Soviet conductor Nikolai Golovanov insisted that the orchestra should re-tune to and play in natural intervals wherever possible.

This is not an easy rendition. It does not simply involve replacing tempered dissonances with natural concords. Everything should be played as originally conceived by the composer. This calls for a good deal of artistic taste on the part of the conductor and the orchestra.

Scriabin's compositions performed with Golovanov conducting sounded exquisite. Many of them have been tape-recorded. You can hear the records in the Scriabin Museum in Moscow.

### THE OLD AND THE NEW

Today classical music is gaining wider popularity. After many decades or even centuries of existence, it has just begun to find its way to the public at large—through radio, L.P.'s and tape-recorders. Moreover, the "good old" music has found an excellent continuation in modern works. Grasped in a new way and ably fused with sharp and bright dissonances, the old harmony of the twelve-interval tempered scale is used by many present-day composers, including a great number of Soviet composers. The trail blazed by Bach is broad and promising, and the overwhelming majority of musicians and musical theorists keep to it.

As attractive, apparently, is another path which can be traced back to Handel, Helmholtz and Scriabin. On this path music will progress by enlarging its territory, by pushing back the frontiers of the traditional tones of the piano and organ. Beyond those frontiers is the virgin land of yet unknown concords; over there, everything is new and yet to be discovered. This path leads to the realm of fresh harmonic beauty and unprecedented freedom of musical creation.

The second approach does not conflict with the first and traditional one. It is rather an extension and elaboration of the same idea. Unfortunately, it has few proponents. This is mainly because the practical realization of the idea seemed sheer day-dreaming until quite recently. Anyhow, today as before a dozen perfect fifths are not equal to seven octaves, and a piano with a thousand keys would be impractical, as would the musical notation to go with it.

For all these objections, however, science and technology are today offering new facilities for a breakthrough in the old tempered system. In collaboration with music, physics is making tools for producing a truly universal musical system. It proceeds not only from the observation and analysis of sound, timbre, mode or harmony you have read about in the previous chapters. It is boldly intervening in the sacrosanctum of music—the very process of musical creation. This, we may say, is an armed intervention, the weaponry being the latest advances in physics, electronics, technology and the searching mind of today's inventor.

We shall get back to the natural musical scale. But before that we shall learn a few things about the simpler (but no less fruitful) fields in which music cooperates with science. Electronics comes first.

CHAPTER SEVEN

\*

# Music from Electricity

Electricity today is a veritable Jack-of-all-trades. It gives light and heat, it feeds, counts, moves and heals. Truly, it is "a sewer, a reaper and a piper—all in one", as the old Russian saying goes.

Electricity is without doubt a promising "piper" today. Many people like the colourful tones of electrophonic instruments. Some of the programmes put out by Radio Moscow (especially variety and dance music) would lose much of their appeal without the Meshcherin Band which has quite a number of electrical musical instruments both Soviet-made and foreign. It is inevitable that electricity, which has invaded science, industry and our homes, should spread into musical art.

What is the principle of an electrical, or electrophonic, musical instrument?

As with any musical sound, the first thing to do is to produce vibrations. While in an ordinary instrument these are the mechanical tremors of the strings, belly, reeds or air columns, in an electrophonic instrument they are oscillations of an electric current. The oscillations are converted, amplified and fed into speakers which transform them into sound waves. That is all there is to it.

As you can see, the electrical "cooking" of musical sounds is not particularly difficult, although it is not so simple as in conventional mechanical instruments. The increased complexity, however, promises a substantial payoff in the greater potentialities of electronic sound. Shrewd inventors spotted these potentialities some time ago. As often happens, however, early inventions were impractical.

### A WHISPERING GIANT

It is less than a century back to those early projects. One of them was the Telharmonium, also known as the Dynamophone, an electric organ invented by the American scientist Dr. Thaddeus Cahill in 1906.

It was an imposing instrument, a veritable musical power station using a number of alternating-current generators producing pure tones. Switches permitted the pure tones to be combined to give notes of any timbre. At that time there were neither amplifiers nor speakers, only rather crude telephones which had just been invented. And it was for telephone lines that Cahill had devised his Telharmonium, so that subscribers, holding the receivers to their ears, could enjoy the unusual music between conversations.

The Telharmonium was so big that a separate building had to be built for it. It would have taken forty railway waggons to carry this mammoth instrument which was bigger than any pipe organ. In spite of its size, however, the giant could only whisper its music to listeners.

To give him his due, Cahill had not done badly. Busoni, a prominent composer of that time, thought well of the Telharmonium. Even today experts have a good word for Cahill's invention.

However, the Telharmonium failed to reach commercial status. And so did other attempts made at that time; none of them carried conviction. In most cases they were just gadgets, ingenious but awkward, more appropriate in a physical laboratory than in the concert-room.

Then electronics came and with it—electronic valves and valve amplifiers which opened up new vistas for electric music.

**THE BIRTH OF ELECTRIC MUSIC**

Picture yourself in bleak, hungry and anxious Petrograd in the autumn of 1919. The counter-revolutionary troops under General Yudenich are closing in on the Russian capital.

On the wet road to Sosnovka, a few miles' ride from Petrograd, you can see a lean young man with his head low, riding a bicycle. Strapped to the carrier are a small travelling case and a cello. The rider turns into the empty yard of the Polytechnic and runs up the long-unswept steps two at a time. Without taking off his coat, he pushes open the door into a small room. Sitting round the table in the room are a few men who are to become prominent figures in science. One of them, a tall man with bright, penetrating eyes, rises to his feet to meet the newcomer.

"Hello, Thérémin. Why are you here?" he says.

"We've blown up the radio station, you know," answers the young man.

"Yes, I know. Don't lose heart. We'll build a new one soon, a hundred times better." Professor Yoffe's voice is cheerful and sure. "Until then you're welcome to work at the new Institute of Engineering Physics."

So Leon Thérémin, chief of the transmitter at the famous radio station in Detskoye Selo, which was blown up in the face of the advancing enemy, became a research worker in the country's first physics institute.

Yoffe assembled a team of active and gifted physicists from the scientists who sided with the revolution. Defying the country's devastation, blockade and poverty, they began experiments and theoretical studies. That was the beginning of Soviet science.

Thérémin was given a huge room with fourteen windows on the second floor of a former military hospital to which the Institute moved in 1920. With the help of laboratory technicians he built two large stoves and, before the iron stove-pipes opening into the windows began discharging smoke and soot, he got down to work.

Yoffe put him to work on capacitive alarm systems and measurements. Before long Thérémin devised a sort of 'radio watchman' which would produce a whistle in headphones should anything approach it. Then followed an instrument for the measurement of the density and dielectric constant of gases by a capacitive method. The instrument could be tuned to the density of a gas like a radio receiver to a sending station. Any change in the density would be indicated by a whistle.

His devices and instruments came at the right time. Both scientists and practical workers welcomed anything new that came along in radio engineering.

The days passed hectically one after another, taken up by research and the spade-work necessary for any new undertaking. As the laboratory settled down, Thérémin's thoughts turned to music, his second profession, which he had nearly forgotten during the stormy revolutionary days. Now it was pushing aside all other thoughts.

Way back, during his university days, Thérémin had graduated from the Petrograd Conservatoire. He had taken great interest in the theory of music and had been a staunch defender of the natural scale.

Not that he found himself having to choose between the two. He would not give up physics; that was certain. Instead, there was the encouraging prospect of making a happy union between physics and music.

In the final analysis, music is a sort of communication, communication between the performer and the listener, Thérémin reasoned. Every musical instrument and the human ear are communications facilities. As a communications engineer, I could try and improve the technique of musical communication in the light of present-day science.

Thérémin knew the strings of his cello were made of monkey gut. Was that not an anachronism in the 20th century? But he was aware that attempts to produce electrical musical instruments had failed. There was a good deal to think over. So it was not at all surprising that he should come upon his remarkable invention.

There it was, his radio capacitometer, set up on the table. In front of the instrument were Thérémin's long, slim fingers which were more accustomed to the black fingerboard of a cello. His fingers disturbed the surrounding atmosphere. The instrument took them for an increase in the density and responded with a low, almost musical tone.

As Thérémin moved his fingers closer to the capacitor, the whistle rose in pitch. When he rocked his fingers as a cellist does, the device produced a warm and beautiful *vibrato*. Then a low, whistling melody came.

"That's an electronic Orpheus' lament," he heard Yoffe's voice from behind. "This thing is worth serious thought, you know. Press on with it, Thérémin."

That was what the young physicist wished to hear.

The next day word went round the place that "our Thérémin plays Gluck on a voltmeter." People flocked to the inventor's room, curious, joking and ready with advice.

It took Thérémin a few days to build his Etherophone (later called the Thérémin and Théréminvox). It was based on the same principle as his 'radio watchman' and density meter.

It had two valve oscillators, one of variable frequency and the other of fixed frequency. One of the capacitor plates in the variable-frequency oscillator was brought outside and connected to a metal rod, the aerial. Moving the hand near the aerial just in the air, without any support, would change the capacitance of the capacitor and with it the frequency of the oscillator. This frequency was combined with that of the fixed-frequency oscillator. As a result, two different frequencies were produced, which physicists call beat frequencies. One of them was the sum of the two original frequencies, and the other was the difference. Now these beats were within the musical range from a few tens to several thousand vibrations per second. What remained to be done was to amplify them and feed them to ... Feed them to what?

In his early experiments Thérémin used ordinary headphones to convert the electric oscillations into sound. But the sound was feeble. The melody could hardly be heard. But the loudspeaker had not yet been invented.

So Thérémin built an oversized earphone as big as a plate and fitted a paper horn to it. The sound became louder, and it could be controlled. The inventor had provided a foot-pedal for this. Now the instrument was ready for public performances.

When in 1921 the 8th All-Russia Electrical Engineering Congress was held in Moscow, Thérémin's electric music was demonstrated and discussed among the technicalities of the historical electrification plan and other scientific discoveries.

### CONQUERING THE CONCERT STAGE

The 8th Electrical Engineering Congress had its sessions in the Polytechnic Museum. There, the Théréminvox was given its first test in public.

The inventor came nervously onto the stage. In the auditorium he saw the famous scientists Krzhizhanovsky, Bonch-Bruevich and Chatelin, and a crowd of noisy, impatient and curious youths. He gave a brief description of his instrument and apologized that he would have to play unaccompanied. The grand which stood on the stage was completely out of tune.

Then a strange music, unlike anything yet heard, floated over the quiet audience. The vibrating electrical tone, now swelling and now falling, was singing familiar airs which sounded new and unusual. There were Russian folk songs, a selection from Tchaikovsky's *The Queen of Spades*, and *The Swan* from Saint-Saëns's *Le carnaval des animaux*.

When he had finished his modest repertoire, the physicist was given the kind of applause that is usually reserved for famous artists.

"Now you should perfect and promote your invention," Yoffe told Thérémin after his debut at the Congress. That gave fresh strength to the inventor.

A few days later he performed in the same auditorium for the general public. And again he was a success. The concert stage had been conquered.

Inside a month Thérémin had mastered a large repertoire, and bills with his name were posted all over Moscow. He performed in local recreation centres, at factories, in colleges, and in governmental offices. His recitals in the Timiryazev Academy and in the Peter Arcades drew huge crowds. The world's first electrophonic instrument had seen the light of day.

But the most pleasant experience Thérémin had at that time was when he performed for Lenin. Here is how the eye-witnesses Fotieva, Thérémin and Fine remember the occasion.

### A RECITAL FOR LENIN

Among the participants in the 8th Electrical Engineering Congress was Akim Nikolayev, a member of the Ministry of Post and Telegraph's Board and chairman of the Radio Council, a sort of government commissar for the growing and expanding radio industry in the Soviet Union. An old-time Bolshevik and an active revolutionary, Nikolayev was at the same time an amateur singer and a devoted music lover. He was able to size up the Théréminvox from both the technical and the musical side. Apparently he thought well of the invention. It is probable that it was through him that Lenin learned about the "electric recital".

Lenin took an interest in the Théréminvox and had the inventor invited to his office in the Kremlin.

So, one day in the winter of 1921, Nikolayev phoned Thérémin and told him that Lenin would like to hear the Théréminvox. He also advised the physicist to take along his 'watchman'.

The inventor went straight to the laboratory where his instruments were kept, arranged for a car to take him, and asked the young electrician Gregory Fine to be his assistant as usual.

It did not take them long to put the instruments, batteries and other things into an old Austin. An hour later the two were in the Kremlin.

Nikolayev gave them a hearty welcome and led them to the small auditorium where they were to perform. The first thing Thérémin saw was a piano. He went over to the instrument, struck a few chords, and found that it was well tuned. He gave a sad sigh. He had thought he would perform in Lenin's office and had not taken a pianist to accompany him. Now it was too late, which was a pity.

He told Nikolayev about his predicament. Nikolayev phoned Lenin, and Lenin found a pianist at once. She was Lydia Fotieva, his secretary. As it turned out, Fotieva had learned to play the piano as a young girl. Later she had had to give up her studies (revolutionary activities and music had not got along well together). Just before the October, 1917 Revolution she had passed her final exams at the Petrograd Conservatoire and so she was qualified as a professional musician.

Lenin called her in and asked whether she could play for Thérémin. Fotieva went to the hall, sat down at the piano and played his repertoire from music with ease. Thérémin was delighted.

Then they set up the electrical equipment, gave it a trial run, and rehearsed for a while. After a few minutes of suspense, the door opened, and Lenin came into the hall, accompanied by Kalinin and other people. Lenin shook hands with Thérémin and his assistant, and the demonstration began.

First Thérémin showed his 'watchman'. As soon as someone put his hand in the 'Keep Away' zone, the device sounded an alarm. Someone tried to cheat the 'watchman' and covered the stretched hand with a cap. Lenin was delighted when the deceit did not work. He watched the demonstration with keen attention. From his remarks the inventor guessed that Lenin had a good knowledge of electrical engineering.

Then came the turn of electric music.

The romance *Do Not Tempt Me Needlessly* was followed by Chopin's nocturne and other pieces.

As Thérémin recalled later, "I felt Lenin was listening to the new instrument with interest. That encouraged me, and I played with enthusiasm. Fotieva's sensitive accompaniment helped a great deal too. When I was about half way through Glinka's *Lark* we had a pleasant surprise. Lenin rose from his chair and came over to the instrument, saying, 'May I have a try?'

"I took Lenin's hand and moved it in front of the aerial, showing him the technique. Lenin grasped it at once and carried the tune to the end himself. 'It's good to think that it has been invented in this country,' he said when we were leaving."

### AT HOME AND ABROAD

It is well known that Lenin encouraged everything new in radio engineering. Several radio stations were built with his support, a world record was set up in long-distance radio communication, and fundamental research in radio engineering began in Russia as early as the Civil War.

Quite naturally, after his visit to the Kremlin Thérémin was given ample support. His 'radio watchman' was mentioned with approval in one of Lenin's letters. The inventor got a permanent railway ticket so that he could tour the country with his Théréminvox. The physicist-musician performed in Nizhny Novgorod, Yaroslavl, Pskov, Minsk and many other cities and gave a total of about one hundred and eighty recitals. And everywhere he was a success.

Gradually the Théréminvox was improved. Yoffe gave Thérémin a loudspeaker, a recent invention at that time. The inventor made radical changes in the circuitry and in addition to the space-controlled Théréminvox devised a fingerboard and a keyboard instrument. Other inventors also began experiments with electric music. Rzhevkin came up with his harmonium. The engineers Gurov and Volynkin built their Violen. Like Thérémin, Gurov was a musician (he played the violin) and at one time worked with him at the radio station in Detskoye Selo near Leningrad.

In the mid-twenties, electric music rallied a large body of support among musicians and scientists. Among the staunchest proponents were Boris Krasin who headed the Music Department at the People's Commissariat of Education, and Professor Garbuzov who had founded the State Institute of the Science of Music. There were quite a number of excellent performers, like Konstantin Kovalsky who is still alive. With every recital their repertoire grew both in scope and size, and the new trend in music came to be a leading topic in newspapers and magazines. These were the first steps of electric music in the Soviet Union. Some time in the future musicologists will painstakingly reconstruct the details of those remarkable events.

Then followed Thérémin's foreign tour in 1927. Stormy applause greeted him in the Berlin Philharmonic Society, the Grande Opera in Paris, the Royal Albert Hall in London, and Carnegie Hall and the Metropoliten Opera House in New York. He won breath-taking fame with the American public. His name was included in the list of twenty-five world celebrities. He performed with Stokowski, Sigetti, Heifetz and Menuhin. Three companies made about three thousand Théréminvoxes and Théréminists. Seven hundred professional théréminvoxists registered with the musicians' trade union.

It is very likely that the triumph of the Soviet physicist-musician spurred the development of electric music in other countries.

### FOR JAZZ AND SERMON

In the twenties and thirties, electrophonic instruments came thick and fast. There were 'purely electrical' instruments like the Théréminvox, the Trautonium invented by Trautwein (Germany) and the Ondes Musicales invented by Martenot (France). There were also electromechanical and electro-optical instruments in which some parts turned, shook or flashed. In the music-halls, variety theatres and concert rooms unusual sounds, whistling, gliding or banging became a standing feature.

Use was also found for the 'light siren' invented by the Soviet scientist Kovalenkov. In this instrument, rotating disks with perforations intercepted a beam of light falling onto photo-cells. The pulsating current from the photo-cells was fed to an amplifier and then to a loudspeaker. In another contraption an endless loop of cine film, with black stripes spaced at intervals, was used to intercept the light beam and give a series of flickers—material for sound-making. The vibrating reeds of a harmonium were also used to break up the light beam.

Laurence Hammond, a watchmaker from Chicago, working on Cahill's old idea, devised an electric organ in which serrated metal disks moved continuously past fixed solenoids—coils of wire round magnets. Every tooth of a disk produced a tone, and in combination they gave a note. There were no electron tubes, except in the amplifier.

The Hammond electric organ soon became popular. It proved good for dancing. Its heart-pinching 'unison *vibrato*' was excellent accompaniment for pop songs. In America the Hammond organ can be found in both churches and homes.

The electric guitar, banjo and mandolin, which came into vogue almost overnight, are simpler still. In an electric guitar there is a pick-up (like the one used in electric record players) fastened to the soundboard. It converts sound vibrations into electric pulses which are amplified and fed to a loudspeaker to produce a strong and rich tone. The famous guitarist Segovia took to the electric guitar at once and used to perform on it.

There were also attempts to use pick-ups on the violin and the grand piano. In 1931 Walter Nernst had the Bechstein grand remodelled at the Physics Institute in Berlin. They removed the soundboard, fitted pick-ups under the strings, and wired them to amplifiers and loudspeakers. Although the timbre changed a little, the increase in strength was considerable. After this, Siemens and Halske soon began making the Neo-Bechstein Pianos.

Inventions came one after another. More new sounds were added, sometimes weird and otherwordly. Inventors spared no effort in advertising their brainchildren. Many of them went so far as to insist that the new instruments were superior to the old which were becoming primitive and old-fashioned by comparison. Some believed that before long electrophonic instruments would completely reorganise the orchestra.

Yet, gradually, the enthusiasm that goes with every innovation gave way to discerning comparison, and weighed and sober judgement. Electric music had entered a conflicting and uneasy formative period.

**PROS AND CONS**

Shortly before the war, a recital was arranged in the Small Hall of the Moscow Conservatoire. The event is still fresh in the memory of electric-music enthusiasts. That day the inventor Ananyev showed his Sonor, a melodic electrophonic instrument. It was a purely electric instrument typical of that time. It had a horizontal fingerboard on which the performer stopped the ribbon of a rheostat. The Sonor could vary timbre. It could even sound like a violin. The recital went on smoothly, and the audience applauded. Encouraged by his success, Ananyev challenged a famous violinist who happened to be sitting in the front row with his violin in his hand. The violinist accepted the challenge. His exquisite Italian violin and the electric newcomer played the same piece in turn. Judging from the reaction of the public, the Sonor emerged victorious—it received a great burst of applause.

That is an instructive story. What conclusion can be drawn from it? Is the Sonor, or anything of its kind, good enough to oust the violin?

Let us assume that you have been asked to arbitrate in the dispute. You will have to take into account these things.

The violin is small and elegant. Its vibrators, resonator and radiator make up a single whole. The electric rival is bulky and awkward. Its parts are built into separate boxes. The paper horn of a loudspeaker does not add elegance, either.

The violin weighs half a pound. The electric instrument is twenty to one hundred times as heavy.

The violin is amazingly simple: a shaped box of wood and four strings. There is nothing in it to puzzle even a child. The electric instrument is an array of electronic valves, coils, capacitors and resistors. You have to be at least a radio amateur and perhaps even a radio expert to say what is what inside it.

The violin needs no external power. The violinist can play anywhere—in the street, in a field, or in a boat on a river. The electric instrument cannot function without a source of electricity.

This is surely enough for us to reject "good-for-nothing" electric substitutes. Indeed, it might appear that the violin is indispensable. For there are things which cannot be improved any more, such as the spoon and the fork.

But let us carry on with our comparison.

The violin covers only the top part of the musical range. For the lower tones (of about the same timbre) you have to use its bigger relatives—the alto, the cello, or the double bass. The electric instrument can replace the whole violin family single-handed.

The violin has an exquisite but not very strong tone. It does not carry far in large halls or outdoors. The electric instrument can play as loudly as you wish.

The violin's timbre is unchangeable. The electric instrument, like a chameleon, can change its tone colour as it plays, now playing like a flute, now like a bassoon or a clarinet, and now altogether differently.

The violin is not at all easy to play. Some believe it is the most difficult of all instruments. It usually takes about fifteen years to turn out a good violinist. The great jokers Ilf and Petrov did not joke when they said, "The violin is a dangerous instrument. You can't play it 'not badly' or 'quite well', as the piano. Mediocre violin-playing is horrible; good playing is mediocre and hardly tolerable. Violin-playing must be superb; only then will it give you pleasure."

Many of the electric instruments, on the other hand, are much simpler to learn than the violin. They are easy to handle and play. So, the comparison is fairly complicated.

**OUT OF THE IDIOM**

If we compare keyboard instruments, both conventional and electric, some of the points will change places.

The pipe organ is a giant weighing many tons and using a great deal of energy. It cannot be moved. It is extremely complicated, fanciful, expensive, and difficult to adjust and tune. There are only three pipe organs in Moscow which organists can use. As often as not the organs are played round the clock; at concerts during the day and in the evening, and at rehearsals at night.

The electric organ is the size of a harmonium. It is simpler and more reliable than the pipe organ. It can easily be adjusted and tuned—by rotating knobs. The timbre can be changed just as easily. The electric organ takes very little energy and its price is low.

Yet the electric organ has a shortcoming which makes it seem unworthy in the eyes of discerning musicians—it cannot yet reproduce pipe tones faithfully. True, it sounds similar to or even very alike the pipe tones, but it has its own sound, a hardly perceptible "electric flavour" which scientists and inventors just cannot get rid of, in spite of all their efforts.

In fact, this is true of all electric instruments. Because of this (and not because of complexity or weight), sensitive musicians after much discussion and many trials, feel compelled to say, "No, it's not quite right, you know. It's out of the idiom."

This is precisely so. The timbres of the symphony orchestra have been perfected over the centuries. Today the tone colours on its rich palette are expertly blended with one another. The composer has learned how to use the symphony orchestra as one huge instrument; he has years of tradition and the skill of instrumentalists to rely on. Through the art of orchestration, that 'musical painting' developed by the great composers Wagner, Rimsky-Korsakov, Berlioz and Debussy, the symphony orchestra today can reproduce the rustle of leaves, the lapping of waves, and the singing of birds. You just cannot mechanically add electric music to this harmony—its charm would be immediately destroyed.

#### SOLOMONIC DECISION

Supposing that instead of making electrophonic instruments imitate conventional ones, we put emphasis on their originality?

Of course, there are different sorts of originality. In pursuit of the short-lived favours of an unexacting public, some people have had bands playing on toilet articles and kitchen utensils. To tell the truth, such stunts are also common in electric music.

Genuine originality is both attractive and promising in any art. It won fame for Thérémin. It promises progress to electric music. Even fairly simple electrophonic instruments sound very like the human voice. By manipulating the timbre controls on the Sonor, you can "say" intelligibly "papa" and "mama". If this can be accomplished by instruments in their infancy, they will surely become good "singers" and "talkers" when they grow up.

To cut a long story short, the arbiter in our imaginary dispute would be well-advised to call upon both sides to stop their feud. Cooperation and mutual assistance are usually far better policies. Let inventors keep imitating known timbres, work to make their instruments simpler, smaller, lighter and more economical and, more important still, let them search for and perfect new, hitherto unknown sound qualities. As to traditional musicians, they should not stick to the old at any cost simply because it is old; they should take an unbiased look at the new and let it find its place in musical art.

Many of the supporters of electric music and musicians of the old school have already accepted these views.

### A FLOOD OF INVENTIONS

In the Soviet Union the fear that music was doomed to "electric degeneration" was ridiculed and dismissed before the war. Since then a painstaking search has been going on for new approaches, better systems, and new effects. The work has already born fruit.

The best instruments, such as the Théréminvox, the Emiriton invented by Ivanov, Dzerzhkovich and Rimsky-Korsakov, the V-8 and the Ekvodin devised by Volodin, have firmly established themselves with both audiences and musicians. The Ekvodin won a Grand Prix at the World Fair in Brussels in 1958. The Americans, delighted by its tone, ordered a large number of Ekvodins in the Soviet Union.

For several years there was a laboratory of broadcasting studio equipment at the U.S.S.R.

Sound Recording Institute in Moscow. That small laboratory produced the now well-known bells which are the call-sign of Radio Moscow, which is heard all over the world. The bells are simple and reliable; a disk rotates slowly, making different contacts, and valve oscillators are energized to give different tones.

The laboratory also experimented with more complicated keyboard instruments, such as the electronic harmonium and the electric tuning-fork piano. Special mention should be made of the electronic bells which have now replaced the heavy metal bells at theatres and in orchestras. The electronic bells, devised by Vasily Maltsev, imitate the well-known timbre so successfully that you can hardly tell them from real bells.

Another man at the laboratory, Saul Korsunsky, M. A., has devised a transistorized electric organ. The instrument, called the Krystadine, is light in weight, powerful and reliable and takes up little space. Its soft and delicate chords sound like those of the harmonium. Leaving out its loudspeakers, the Krystadine takes only three watts of energy, or as much as a flash-light lamp.

Semiconductors, those wonderful crystals which have ousted conventional electronic valves, promise a great breakthrough in electric music. Electrophonic instruments can now be made compact, reliable and economical. The day may come when an electric violin will work from a dry-cell the size of a button or from the light illuminating it. Still greater hopes are pinned on micromodules, another miracle-worker from the rapidly developing field of electronics. Using microcircuitry techniques you can squeeze an amplifier into a micromodule the size of a pin-head and package complex circuits into the space of a thimble. There is plenty of scope for the inventor. And this, as you will see later, is exactly what he needs, for electrophonic instruments are becoming increasingly sophisticated.

### TONE COLOUR AT CHOICE

The layman might say that it is not at all difficult to devise new timbres by electric means; with all those oscillators, amplifiers and filters, non-existent in the 1920's, the inventor's job is simply to put pure tones together, and that is all there is to it. However, it is not quite so simple as that.

You will remember that the beauty of any note depends on its harmonic content, i.e., the presence of partial tones or harmonics. This feature is inherent in conventional instruments. Their strings or air columns vibrate as a whole, in halves, thirds, fourths and so on, producing tones with frequencies which are two, three, four or more times as high as that of the fundamental tone.

In electrical systems, oscillations are governed by other laws. A simple valve oscillator produces no partials at all. They can only be obtained by having an oscillator circuit for each one. Without this, the note is weird rather than beautiful.

Partials can be added to the fundamental tone of an electrophonic instrument on the basis of a mathematical theorem proved by the French scientist J. B. Fourier in 1822. For our purposes we may state it as follows: a series of simple harmonic (or purely sinewave) vibrations can be combined into a complicated periodic vibration. Conversely, any periodic vibration can be analyzed into such a series.

You can see an excellent illustration to Fourier's Theorem on the sound track of a cine film (recorded by the Shorin or variable-area method). The sounds are presented as graphs which clearly show their waveform. The violin is represented by a sawtooth curve, and the clarinet by what looks like a line of inverted U's carelessly written. A far more complicated graph is obtained when the violin and the clarinet play together. Later on we shall discuss the sound track of films in greater detail. For the time being it is sufficient to state that Fourier's Theorem offers two efficient methods for synthesizing "live" notes on electrophonic instruments.

In the first method the oscillator circuit can be so arranged that, instead of simple harmonic vibrations, it will generate periodic vibrations of the desired harmonic content and waveform. The main handicap at present lies in the fact that existing oscillator circuits cannot yet shape just any waveform easily. That is why their timbres lack richness and variety. These, however, are temporary difficulties, and they will be overcome with further progress in electronics.

In the other method, which is actually used, simple harmonic vibrations of different single frequencies, or tones, are generated separately and then compounded in the desired proportion. By synthesizing tones of the true or natural scale, we could obtain superb timbres. However, this method, too, suffers from limitations, especially when it comes to instruments which have to be tuned in equal temperament.

The point is that notes in equal temperament differ from those of the true or natural scale. Since, however, the notes of electric instruments are compounded from natural tones additional oscillators would have to be provided to make up for the discrepancy. Because of this, the electric instrument would become prohibitively complicated. This is where semiconductors and micromodules come in.

### TRIFLES COUNT

Strictly speaking, tone quality depends not only on harmonic content. The beginning and end of a note must also be considered. You would hardly recognize a piano note without its beginning, or attack, as it is called.

A German professor carried out an interesting experiment. He had a group of musicians listen to different instruments whose notes had been made 'attackless'. The musicians found it very difficult to guess which note was sounded by what instrument.

From this story it is clear how important attack is. Sometimes it must be gradual, as in the accordion, and sometimes sharp, as in the piano. In an electric instrument, therefore, there must be some sort of control—perhaps magnetic or inductive, to vary the attack at will.

Nor should we overlook the rise and fall of a note. A piano note, after it is struck, varies in loudness and harmonic content differently from a note in any other instrument. And again, in an electrical instrument there must be a device to control both loudness and quality at will, a feature non-existent in the piano.

Finally, there is the soft, uncontrolled noise that accompanies the sound of all conventional instruments: the sound of fingers touching the keys, the resin of the bow sucking at the strings, and so on. This is not just noise. No. It makes an instrument sound live and warm. On the other hand, because of its purity, electric sound has a cool and abstract quality about it. Of course, you can warm up and enliven electric sound, but it is not simple to do. You have to add many more components to the circuitry, making it very involved.

There are many more problems to tackle, small and big, simple and tricky. All of them call for close study. Sometimes what at first appears to be a mole-hill grows into a big mountain from which you get an unobstructed view of the things to come.

This is exactly what happened with the noise-phone, an interesting electric instrument devised by Igor Simonov of the Sound Recording Institute.

## NOISE MADE TO ORDER

The stone was set rolling when Simonov thought of warming up the tone of one of his instruments which sounded too otherwordly to him. He tried several approaches and finally selected the 'white noise generator', a source of random fluctuations of electric energy which have no definite frequency. When mixed with musical sounds, white noise made them live and warm in quality.

The noise was so pleasant that the inventor thought of leaving out the sound generator altogether and of carrying on the melody with the noise generator alone. The idea might seem strange at first glance, but it is based on a firm footing. By passing white noise through a suitable radio filter, you can catch random fluctuations which lie within the desired frequency range. In this way, you can produce sounds very close to musical sounds. That was how Simonov came upon 'music production by noise selection'.

Suppose you dump together all the sounds that exist in the world around you: the blasts of explosions, the roar of waves, the whistles of factories, the din of machines, symphonic music and arias. Now you want to pick something out of this cacophony. This is roughly what Simonov planned to.

As soon as he had built his instrument, it was used to imitate the howling of the wind. If the reader has seen the film *The Forty First*, he must remember the continuous whistling of the wind in the opening scenes. The wind was imitated by Simonov's noisephone. The performer manipulated the controls of the noisephone and the wind rustled, hissed, rang, rumbled and sang boisterously. It gave a faithful imitation of a wild and raging steppe storm.

The electronic wind also proved to be a good singer. In the same film it sang several tunes, an effect unattainable with any conventional instrument. The singing wind was also played on the radio, and there were a good many enthusiastic letters from listeners.

With further improvements in 'noise selection', Simonov has been able to turn his instrument into a source of all sorts of sound effects. Now it is a sophisticated piece of automatic apparatus with keys, switches and a metal fingerboard.

The inventor sits down at his instrument, turns on a switch, and you can hear the warbling of a nightingale, the continuous singing of a skylark, the twitter of a chiff-chaff, and the wooing and cooing of some unknown birds. Then he presses a key and turns a knob and you can hear a blow, an explosion, or a swelling rumble as if a rocket is shooting off its launching pad. Pressure on yet another key and rotation of another knob changes the sound picture again; now you can hear unearthly music from a fairy land.

Some of the effects of the noisephone are so unusual that you can hardly describe them. Many are valuable discoveries for films and radio productions. As the film director Ptushko wrote, "A good many sound effects have been recorded with this excellent instrument: tanks on the march, blasts, gun-fire, the beat of the drum, etc. With other methods, these sounds would have taken much more time and effort to record. On the noisephone, they were imitated faithfully and with ease."

The quest for new musical qualities is going on. More and more sounds are being added to the electrophonic repertoire. Today you will hardly find a single film not using them. Electrophonic instruments have become inseparable from light music, radio productions and the stage. Quite a number of composers, especially the younger ones, eager to use all that is new and exciting, are writing for them.

CHAPTER EIGHT

*

# The Wonders of Sound Recording

On March 11, 1878, Fellows of the French Academy of Sciences heard Edison's first phonograph for the first time. The famous inventor had sent an assistant who was turning a wax-coated cylinder, so that a stylus moved over the grooves in the wax. This imparted vibrations to a diaphragm and the machine reproduced the few words that had been recorded, in a greatly distorted yet human voice.

All of a sudden Boulliot, a venerable old man, stopped the demonstration and shouted at the technician showing the phonograph:

"You scoundrel, stop kidding us with your ventriloquistic tricks!"

But what the poor old man thought was a trick soon proved its honesty.

In 1888 Emile Berliner, an engineer, invented the 'gramophone', the type of phonograph which uses disk records. His first disk is now in the U.S. National Museum in Washington. Within a few years the gramophone spread round the world like an epidemic. Disk records were made by the thousand, of poor quality and very noisy, yet they invariably enraptured the listeners.

Many forms have been tested for the gramophone, and many materials have been tried for the disks. There has also been a humorous side to the development. At the beginning of this century, a confectioner's shop in St. Petersburg, Russia, turned out gramophone disks made of chocolate. You could both listen to and eat the music.

The gramophone of today uses a sapphire stylus which does no harm to the sound grooves on the disk, and excellent pick-ups which are sensitive and light in weight. Drives, turntables and changers perform superbly. With L.P. disks and high-fidelity record players you can hear, without leaving your home, the best symphony orchestras playing so realistically that if you close your eyes you cannot tell there are no musicians present.

In the 1920's several methods were introduced for optical sound recording on film. The first step is to photograph the sound. This is done in various ways. Amplified currents from the microphone may feed a gaseous discharge lamp so that its light output varies in step with the sound. This light is projected onto a moving film; when it is developed there is a strip of varying density. In playing the sound back, a beam of light shines through this strip as the film moves through the projector, and the light passing through the strip varies in step with the original sound. As it falls on a photo electric cell, the current is amplified, fed into a loudspeaker, and we have a reproduction of the sound that went into the microphone. These are called 'variable-density' methods of sound recording. There are also methods by which a sound track of white and black is produced on the film so that the white varies in width. This is the 'variable-area' method of sound recording. For all their seeming complexity, sound-on-film methods have proved very reliable. They heralded the doom of silent pictures.

In the 1930's and 1940's, further steps were made in sound recording by magnetic means. The principle is embodied in the tape recorder now found throughout the world. It uses a plastic tape covered with a coat of ferromagnetic material which looks very much like rust. In magnetic recording sound is converted into variations of electric current, and these reorient the metallic oxide particles in the coating on the tape. When the tape is played back the process is reversed.

### A VISIT TO THE SOUND STUDIO

When the radio announcer says that a symphony by Beethoven is about to be played, this does not mean that an orchestra is actually present in the studio, waiting for the conductor to wield his baton. Nothing of the kind. The musicians may be anywhere, even at home over their cups of tea. If you were to drop in at the studio at that time, you would only see the announcer and the engineer at tape recorders. Their disks carry brown magnetic tape on which the symphony has been recorded to the last note. Instead of a conductor's inspiring baton, the music begins with pressure on a push-button.

Yet the symphony was performed by a real orchestra all the same—a day, a week or, perhaps, a month ago. The musicians met at the studio many times, going through the difficult passages over and over again. And while the "canned music" was being prepared, everything was being done to make it sound as good as, or even better than, "live" music in a concert-hall. The conductor and orchestra were helped in this by a sound engineer well versed in both music and acoustics. He told the musicians where to sit and his assistants where to place microphones slung from long booms. During the performance the sound engineer sat at his control desk, listening to the music and turning the knobs. He could control the loudness and even the quality of the various groups of instruments.

Today the job of the sound engineer at a recording or radio studio is inseparable from that of the performing artists. The reason is simple. Most music today is heard "canned", i.e., recorded on tape or disks. The equipment at the disposal of the sound engineer is continuously being improved so that the recording can sound even more realistic.

Composers, too, are keeping pace with progress in sound recording and reproduction. Even before the war Sergei Prokofiev skilfully utilized the effects of the then imperfect optical sound recording for the music to the film *Ale-*

*xander Nevsky*. He singled out the horns by having them played right into the microphone. In the same way he built up the sound of the bassoon. He had the chorus and the trumpeters perform in separate studios so that the loudness and quality could easily be controlled separately.

Today the control techniques of sound recording have become unbelievably sophisticated. On top of this the sound engineer can easily process the sound already recorded by filtering, mixing or superimposing. In a way, his work resembles that of restoring valuable old paintings.

**LENIN'S VOICE**

Some years ago a major event took place in the Soviet sound-recording industry. Long-playing updated records of Lenin's seven speeches were released. Those who had heard the old records had a pleasant surprise. The new records were free from the sharp hissing sound, Lenin's voice had become much clearer, and all the words were now intelligible. In the opinion of those who had heard Lenin in person, even the most minute inflexions of his voice had been restored.

It was a difficult job. The hardest to tackle was the scratch noise which was unavoidable in the old sound-recording technique. Because of it, whole sentences were sometimes difficult to make out. A commission set up by the Marxism-Leninism Institute had required that Lenin's voice be restored with maximum fidelity. And the requirement was met.

Success was for a large part due to special devices developed for the purpose. One of them was a noise suppressor worked out by Vladimir Weinbaum, an engineer. This is a kind of radio filter which "weeds" noise rather than cuts off the higher audio frequencies. It does so automatically, adapting itself to the changing situation and without affecting the useful signal.

Work is still going on on the old records of Lenin's speeches. More updated disks are to appear soon, treated at a new and higher level of technical skill. There is no doubt that they will be another major success for the enthusiasts.

A similar technique has been used to update rare musical records.

#### UPDATED CHALIAPIN

The heavy, exquisitely decorated case held only one gramophone record. It was a very old one, scratched and worn out. The title read: *The Seven Sons-in-Law*. A Russian folk song. Singer: Chaliapin.

The owner carefully picked up the disk by the edges and placed it on a record player. Through noisy hissing, crackling and clicking you could hear the amazing bass of young Chaliapin. At times you could only guess rather than hear his voice which was drowned either by scratches or by the nasal refrain of a poor choir.

Then the noise suppressor was turned on, filters tuned, and tape recorders started. A second tape recording was made from the first, and then a third. The voice now came from the loudspeaker velvety and sonorous, as if the singer were alive. But Alexei Arshinov, the engineer in charge, was dissatisfied. The record could not be used yet. Why? Because the accompanying choir had also been bolstered. Now their howling was spoiling the song even more than before. What a nuisance! Could anything be done?

Arshinov had an idea: "What if Chaliapin were to sing with a good choir, such as the Soviet Army Ensemble?"

Difficult as it was, the idea was quite feasible and was put into practice.

The Soviet Army Ensemble fitted their refrain to Chaliapin's recording so nicely that you could hardly distinguish them either in tonality, rhythm or manner. Then a separate recording of the ensemble's performance was made. Next Georgy Dudkevich, a sound engineer, came into action. He removed the old accompaniment and fitted the new one, keeping the same loudness. So Chaliapin's record was brought back to life. Today it is among the most valuable possessions of the Radio Committee's sound recordings.

People from the U.S.S.R. Sound Recording House have also "resurrected" the marvellous voices of Sobinov and Nezhdanova. In some cases the poor accompaniment has been replaced by first-class orchestras.

Today a soloist is often separated from the orchestra in new recordings. First the soloist is recorded and then the orchestra, and finally the sound engineer mixes them together. And you may be sure that the two will never wander apart, nor will the soloist be drowned by the trumpets or the timpani.

### A ONE-MAN ORCHESTRA

Can one pianist play a piece for eight pianos?

Yes, he can—in our age of electronics. And he can do this with his own hands on a single piano. The only "extra" he will need is two tape recorders.

If you were that pianist, you could do the trick as follows. With one of the tape recorders running you play one piano part. Then you put on headphones, listen to the first recording, and play the second piano part so that both parts fit in and are recorded on a second tape machine. Now you listen to the second recording, play the part of a third piano, and both are recorded on the first tape. Then a fourth record is made by mixing the third record, and so on.

This sound-on-sound technique, although it takes a long time, may be very useful in some cases. Thus the inventor of a new electrophonic instrument can give it a trial run in a non-existent orchestra consisting of ten such pieces.

If you have enough patience and can play different instruments, you can use this technique to become a one-man orchestra. There are tape machines which produce records of different instruments in turn on different tracks of the same tape. When the sound is played back all the tracks are reproduced simultaneously. Although this machine makes the job easier, it still calls for truly German punctuality (incidentally the first such machine was built in Germany).

This technique holds out special promise for singers. One person can sing the parts of a whole choir. Just imagine a choir of one hundred Galli-Curcis! But we have gone too far here. The famous singer would have to spend fifty hours preparing a three-minute song. None of the famous singers would think this worthwhile. It does seem practical, however, to 'mix together' duets, trios, quartets, and even septets or octets with the added attraction of a good orchestra. In fact, there are already singers who are using this technique on the stage. Ima Soumak, for example, sings a 'duet' with herself in some of her performances—with great success.

### AN ECHO IN A ROOM

As a child you probably enjoyed listening to echoes near the edge of a wood. You shouted—and soon heard a faint, parroting reply. You know why this happens. The wood sends back the sound waves reaching it, and you can hear your own voice. The echo is particularly good in the mountains. Their stone sides absorb very little sound energy, and the echo comes back loud and clear.

Can there be an echo in a room?

Everyone knows how a voice resounds in a large, empty room—quite unlike in the open air. This is what acousticians call 'reverberation'. Even though it is not exactly a 'room echo', it is very much like it. The walls, ceiling and floor in a room are very close to each other, and the reflected sound travels back and forth very rapidly. Because of this, we cannot hear separate words or syllables in the echo. Instead, there is a blur of sounds in the case of speech, and a sustained note in the case of music.

Two rooms may be of the same size and shape, yet music may sound rich, brilliant and full of life in the first and dull, flat and dead in the second. This is because of a difference in reverberation. In the first room it helps the performers, and in the second it hinders them.

During the opening ceremony at a newly built college the principal rose to the rostrum, began his speech and fell silent, embarrassed. Instead of speech, there was an unintelligible mixture of sounds. Built by an engineer who cared little about architectural acoustics, the conference hall proved too reverberant. When any syllable was spoken, a train of preceding ones was still echoing round the hall. The audience hardly got a single word.

An example of a room with an ideal amount of reverberation is the Hall of Columns in Moscow. Both voice and music seem to be carried by the air itself, and become rich and full. The secret lies in the well proportioned and well positioned columns, and other architectural details of the Hall.

Present-day architects have a clear idea of how a room should be designed for excellent hearing. They make finned ceilings, ledges, and columns. Before the actual construction, tests are carried out on models. Special care is taken in designing sound studios because their acoustics is a very delicate matter. Among other things, rooms must be acoustically different for speech and for music. In fact, they must be different for different music. But if we blindly followed the advice of acousticians for high-fidelity sound recording, we would have to build separate studios for orchestras, choirs, pianists, violinists and singers.

Fortunately there is a very simple and effective way out. In the Soviet Union it was suggested by the engineer Georgy Goldberg at the U.S.S.R. Sound Recording Institute.

### AN ELECTRIC ECHO

The tape recorder is playing one of Glinka's romances, sung by Zara Dolukhanova. The tune, caressing and sincere, is flowing freely and unrestrained, as it would sound on a river bank in the quiet of the evening. Now the surroundings change, and the song is coming from a high grotto. It resounds under stone arches, floating slowly away and spreading in the labyrinth. Then it breaks into the open again, with the same unrestrained quality as before.

Do you think Zara Dolukhanova walked as she sang? No, of course not. She sang in a well sound-proofed studio. Then the sound engineer processed the record on a piece of apparatus called a reverberator. The echo, the resounding grotto and the open-field quality were all added by rotating controls on its panel.

This reverberator is basically a tape recorder in which an endless loop of tape moves past a recording head, several play-back heads and an erasing head. The recording head takes down every note of the record being made at the same time as the main tape machine. The playback heads reproduce it, each with a certain delay, and the note appears in the main record as an echo, adding richness and fullness to the sound. The reverberator may be adjusted so that every echo is a bit weaker than the preceding one or so that the echoes come faster or more slowly after each other, as if the distance from imaginary reflecting walls were changing. Instead of a tape loop, a disk may be used. The "echo" is removed at the erasing head, and the tape is ready to be used again.

Thus the reverberator works as a good substitute for a large hall and can produce an echo, a peal or a rattle—it is a sort of invisible sound prop. An experienced and imaginative sound director can work miracles with it.

A few years ago Radio Moscow broadcast the production of a fairy tale, *The Courageous Gonza*. In the tale the road speaks in a non-human voice. It spoke through a reverberator, and its voice was anything but human—sprawling and spreading far and wide. In the same production a female sextet was made to sound like a choir of a thousand.

With a reverberator you can make the small voice of an indifferent singer sound perfect. Or on a gramophone disk you can add an accompaniment of violins playing in a reverberant hall to the part of a singer singing outdoors.

This technique is firmly established in recording light music. With due care and tact, an electric echo can be added to symphonic records. Classical music thus comes by a new quality.

Although it is a relative newcomer, the reverberator has become an indispensable tool to every sound director.

### BETTER THAN LIVE MUSIC

Suppose you have an ordinary radio receiver. You turn it on, and music comes out of it. You know and like the music—it sounds superb. You close your eyes and concentrate. It's fine, but the effect is not the same as when you sit in a concert-hall. There the music, powerful and entrancing, rushes on you like a huge wave, engulfing you from all sides. At home the sound comes from one point only—the loudspeaker hidden behind a silk screen. This is not enough to make your pleasure complete, even though the loudspeaker may be of the best quality. You want to feel the orchestra playing in front of you, with the cellos on one side, the French horns answering from the other side, and the organ roaring somewhere above them. You want an illusion of breadth and depth of sound.

There is nothing in this that cannot be fulfilled by modern electronics. The technique that does the trick is known as stereophonics.

The idea of stereophonics is this. The music of an orchestra is picked up by two or more microphones spaced a certain distance apart. A separate channel of amplification and transmission or recording runs from each microphone. At the receiving or reproducing end of the system separate channels feed the respective loudspeakers. Even with two loudspeakers you get the illusion of three-dimensional sound. With properly placed speakers, a performance in a large cathedral can be realistically re-created and enjoyed in a small room. Just close your eyes, and each sound will seem to come from its correct place.

Stereophonics has come a long way since the first attempts. Today stereo broadcasts, stereo disks and stereo tape have all become commonplace in everyday life. A good many FM-VHF stations transmit stereophonic programmes on a regular basis. Special systems have been devised for making four-track stereophonic recordings on magnetic tape. Stereophonic long-playing records have the right- and left-hand audio signals engraved on the two sides of each groove. Stereophonic sound systems for motion pictures, especially wide-screen and panoramic films, use as many as seven channels or even more. Experiments have been carried out with as many as twelve channels. The old problem of where to seat the musicians is solved without them.

Stereophonics, like every art, has stunt-men of its own. By placing speakers in suitable positions they can make a soloist sound as if he is running about the stage. True, this 'ping-pong-ball' effect, as it is called, often comes about spontaneously when the sound engineer is not very experienced. But there are also genuinely artistic effects which no orchestra can obtain.

With sound montage, updating, superposition, reverberation and stereophonics, "canned music" can be even better than live music! This is like the photographer who says he can "make you look better than in real life".

Sometimes, however, sound control is used to distort, or rather process, sound.

**PROCESSED VOICES**

There is hardly a single summer park in the Soviet Union without a 'laughing room'. Its equipment is simple—an assortment of distorting mirrors. It is amusing to see yourself stretched out into a pole or compressed into a pan-cake.

Sound, too, can be stretched or compressed for special effects. If you play back a tape at half the speed at which it was recorded, the tones will become longer and, therefore, lower in pitch. A tenor will sound like a bass or a baritone. If you play back a tape faster than the recording speed, the tones will become shorter and, therefore, higher in pitch. A bass will now sound like a treble. Not that there is any artistic value in such a transformation. Yet such stunts are sometimes useful.

A few years ago Radio Moscow broadcast a production of *The Adventures of Buratino*. It was a one-man affair, with the actor Nikolai Litvinov playing all the parts. Where necessary, his voice was expanded, compressed or superimposed on itself by a tape machine. This gave the bass of Karabas-Barabas, the high-pitched "wooden" voice of Buratino himself, and his famous song. Since then this technique, pioneered in the Soviet Union by Rose Yoffe, has been used in many other programmes.

A multitude of sound-control techniques have been developed by the electronic music studio at the Cologne Broadcasting Station. One of them works like this. Suppose there is a composition written in very rapid tempo and difficult to perform. For tape recording the musicians play at a slow tempo and an octave below that required. During play-back the tape is made to move at twice the recording speed. Because of this, all the tones rise in pitch by exactly an octave, and thus sound exactly as they should. The tempo, too, is doubled, and is as it was conceived by the composer. It is very simple and easy.

Why on earth should the piece be played at half the tempo if the tape is played back at twice the normal speed, you might ask. Would it not be simpler to play the music as it was written by the composer?

It is all done to make the performance cleaner. A fast passage played at a slow tempo can be played with greater precision and confidence. Nuances, too, can be better rendered in slow playing. A fast play-back restores the passage in all its masterly brilliance. Or does it?

#### AN ELECTRONIC CONDUCTOR

At one time there was a whole orchestra at the Cologne Studio, performing this way. It must have been a funny sight to see the musicians and conductor hardly move their hands. Something like the slow-motion effect in a film taken at high speed.

To be able to perform like that the musicians needed a good deal of imagination. For they had to perform what they were not hearing. Could this transformation be perfect? Could neat playing replace the expressive inspiration of a genuine virtuoso? Which of the two prevailed: beauty or originality?

There was little beauty in the performance, I'm afraid. The musical quality was changed beyond recognition if for no other reason than that the beginning of each note was compressed to half its normal duration.

The Cologne Studio has been more successful with a sound-manipulating machine developed by Springer, an engineer. With this machine you can vary the speed and also the rhythm and dynamics of the original composition at will.

Basically it is a multitrack tape recorder with closely spaced play-back heads. As it moves the tape touches all the heads at the same time. At each particular moment, however, only one head picks up the signal. This is because the heads are energized in turn, one after the other. If the "wave" of the heads coming into action catches up with the tape, the tones are slowed down; if it lags behind, the tones are speeded up. Since the tape moves at constant speed with respect to the heads you need not fear any 'wow' or 'flutter', that abominable howling inevitable when the speed of the tape itself varies. By using the controls for the duration and volume of individual tones you can in effect conduct music that was performed long ago at any other tempo—which is another miracle worked by electronics.

Performing artists can also benefit from the Springer machine. They can now play any music, no matter what degree of virtuosity it demands. This includes some of Paganini's pieces which have so far frustrated the best violinists, and a few of Beethoven's and other composers' works, as difficult in technique. Although artificial, this is true virtuosity.

The Springer machine is certainly a boon to conductors. It relieves them of the necessity of spending time and effort in endless rehearsals. Many of the nuances can now be polished in advance, using any recording of the music.

**TAPED ACTUALITY**

Somewhere in the 1920's or 1930's a good many composers believed they could add vitality to their music by including the sounds of a broken window-pane, a lathe, or a gun shot. One publicity-seeking composer wrote a concerto for typewriter and orchestra, and another a quartet for car horns. The best such music could earn was a smile. Usually it left the audience indifferent or angry. In fact, this was not music. This is not to say, however, that there is no room for sound effects in good music.

Drums, timpani and rattles do not produce musical sounds, yet no orchestra can possibly do without them. However, these traditional percussion instruments sometimes prove unable to express all the noises filling our everyday life.

In his background music to a battle scene in the film *Alexander Nevsky*, Sergei Prokofiev reinforced drums and timpani with some "box from the Moscow Film Studio", as he wrote in the score.

Young Shostakovich wove sound effects into the music and action of *The Plan*, one of the first Soviet 'talking pictures'. The culmination of the plot is accentuated by the rising whistle of a steam turbine undergoing a test. As the test approaches the critical stage the turbine picks up speed, and the whistling of the steam grows sharper and more penetrating. No music could equal this simple sound in the drama expressiveness and feeling of suspense it conveys.

As sound recording has progressed, both the cinema and theatre have become steady users of what is technically known as taped actuality —tapes with the sounds of waves breaking against the shore, rain falling on the ground, factory whistles hooting in the morning, and crowds a thousand strong yelling at the tops of their voices. A good deal of use is made of the noisephone described in the preceding chapter, the reverberator, and other sound-control devices. The composer Andrei Volkonsky injected processed sound effects into his music for George Bernard Shaw's *Saint Joan* when it was staged by a Moscow theatre. Taped actuality has come to stay in the theatre.

In fact, non-musical sounds have become an integral part of much good music. They are serving and will continue to serve as a documentary and even as an artistic complement to it.

But, as is the case with any artistic technique, imagination is not everything. The things that really count are taste, talent and mastery. Without them, beauty departs, leaving behind sheer senseless stunt-seaking.

CHAPTER NINE

\*

## Dr. Sholpo's Dream

Some artists, instead of a pencil and a sheet of paper, use a pair of scissors, a can of glue and a lot of photographs to make their pictures. Their technique is known as 'montage'. If a montage artist needs, say, a black star, he finds a photograph of a man wearing a black jacket, cuts a star out of it, and glues it in place. If he needs an eye or a nose, the procedure is the same.

What if he needs a tip-tilted nose and the photographs, to spite him, show only straight ones? An experienced montage-maker will know what to do. He will soak a photograph of a straight nose in a chemical solution and distort it to his liking. That is all there is to it. The technique is simple, but boring. It would be more attractive to draw the picture, wouldn't it?

A similar technique is in use in sound recording. Tape or optical recordings are cut, reversed or processed in some other way, and then spliced to give a musical picture altogether different from the source material. But, by analogy with photographic montage, the question suggests itself, would it not be simpler to abandon this chopping and mincing of music and to draw sounds instead? Would this not open up new musical possibilities?

"Drawing sounds" does sound a bit strange, doesn't it? There was an artist who used to draw sonatas and rhapsodies as mysterious curves and circles on paper and then quietly went mad.

But do not jump at conclusions. This world is full of amazing but true things.

### IN THE LECTURE HALL

One evening in the autumn of 1939 a tall, slightly stooping man with a mocking look in his penetrating eyes rose to the rostrum in a lecture hall of Moscow University. He was to speak on graphic sound, his invention.

He spoke with rare sarcasm. His biting remarks sounded as if he was answering some invisible opponents. He was eager to convince the audience that his unorthodox and daring ideas held out great promise to music. Graphic or hand-drawn sounds, he said, offer an inexhaustible source of tone colours, virtuosity unattainable by any human virtuoso, and freedom for the composer from performers to bring his music to life.

Then the lecturer demonstrated his invention. He used the Overture to *Carmen*. Familiar to the last note since childhood, it now sounded differently in the loudspeakers. Some unknown trumpets and strange bells had changed the old music, giving it a new quality. There was the famous *Valkyries' Flight* which filled the auditorium with whirling sounds. There were other old pieces. But in each there was something unusual.

At the end of his lecture the man answered the notes he had received from the audience. One of them read, "Where can I go to learn your art?" When the question was read aloud, the hall chuckled. But the lecturer took the question in earnest.

"If you mean that, you need a working knowledge of three subjects: acoustics, electronics and music. We need people who are musicians and, at the same time, are knowledgeable about engineering, physics, mathematics, and physiology," he said.

The lecturer was the late Yevgeny Sholpo, Doctor of the History of Art, a musicologist and inventor, the unquestionable founder of an art now called synthetic music.

### THE LEONARDO DA VINCI SOCIETY

As a young man, Sholpo was a member of the Leonardo da Vinci Society. The Society had set itself the ambitious goal of giving music a radical scientific overhaul. The young and hotheaded da Vincists were eager to accomplish many things: to revolutionize acoustics, to improve the musical scale, to unravel the psychological secrets of musical performance, to invent new musical instruments, and to free music from musicians. Naturally, there was a lot of riding of high horses and cock-fighting against "antiquated" classical traditions. As Sholpo wrote later, "It did not occur to us that the musical art had many valuable traditions which must be preserved and from which we could proceed."

Because of a glaring discrepancy between the lofty aims and an empty purse, the Society was mainly busy making fantastic plans and indulging in idle dreams. At that time Sholpo wrote a science-fiction story, *The Enemy of Music*. It features a mechanical orchestra run by the composer himself, playing without musicians but better than any orchestra with them. There is a detailed description of the machine, perhaps too detailed for a literary work. But reading it now, you cannot help admiring the young inventor's wealth of ideas and foresight. Just imagine that way back in 1917 Sholpo came upon the idea of what is known today as an electronic music synthesizer (don't be frightened—this will be explained later). The author describes the basic sounds in the machine being derived from electromagnetically maintained tuning forks and processed by semiconductor devices known today as photoresistors, but not known at that time.

The author does not stint his praise of the machine. He makes it play any conceivable chords and passages. Instead of the equal temperament of the pianoforte, it uses a continuous scale on which only perfect harmonics and consonances are produced so that timbre, harmony and orchestration all blend into a single entity.

But it was only a dream, even though an alluring one. There was no hope of realizing it. At that time the only mechanical facilities for musical performance were the piano player and the automatic piano. And Sholpo worked stubbornly, trying to improve the mechanical players.

His daring project of a mechanical orchestra remained remote, unfeasible and illusory until the advent of optical sound recording. 'Talking pictures' changed everything for Sholpo.

**GRAPHIC SOUND**

Let us go back to sound recording by the variable-width method (known in the Soviet Union as the Shorin method after its inventor). The film has a continuous black strip with a serrated edge. Briefly, it is produced in this way. The varying current from the microphone alters the length of the slit illuminated by a constant light source. When the film is passed behind the slit, which opens and closes in step with the sound being recorded, an exposed track is left on the film. After developing, it will be seen as a continuous strip with one edge serrated. Each instrument produces serrations of a particular shape so that those made by the flute will differ from those of the clarinet or the violin.

It was this sound track that Sholpo saw when he and Arseny Avraamov, an old acquaintance of his and another da Vincist, dropped in at Shorin's laboratory in the autumn of 1929.

As the inventor explained his method, one of the visitors (just who it was neither Sholpo nor Avraamov could recollect later) had the amazingly simple idea of drawing the sound track by hand, without having a single instrument played. The sound track could be drawn on the film in Indian ink, he reasoned, and the film passed through Shorin's reproducer. The sounds reproduced will be ones that have never been played. It will no longer be just sound recording, but the creation of sound. It might well be a promising start to the 'self-playing orchestra', he wound up triumphantly.

Indeed, the sound tracks can be cut in any way we please. We can cut them to imitate the tone of a violin or a clarinet. Or we can draw ones which give sounds which have never been heard on land or sea.

Moreover, we can draw any melody with whatever natural intervals we please, not necessarily on the traditional scale of the pianoforte. For there are no keys or other mechanical features to limit our choice. The density of serrations and, consequently, the pitch of the tone can be varied at will. By drawing several tracks one above the other, we can produce smooth concords never heard before.

Such was the breath-taking perspective Sholpo and his colleagues saw with their mind's eye. Sholpo, the most effusive, was eager to test the idea at once. But how? The serrations were so small that they could not be drawn with a

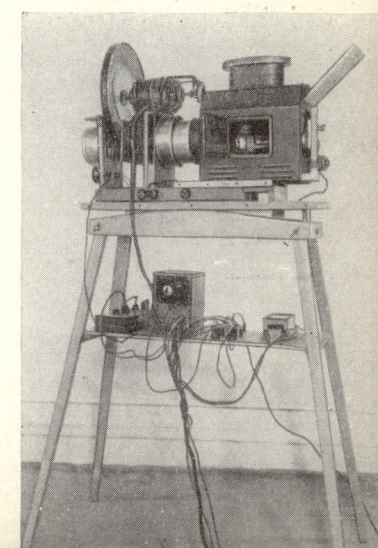

Thérémin's instruments.
a—the Théréminvox (1923); b—the Illumovox (1926)

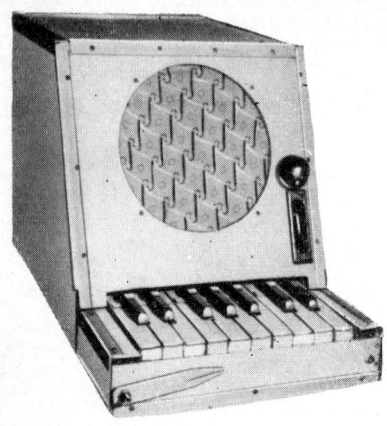

*The rhythmicon, a device for studies into musical rhythms*

*The Marconi-Stille recording apparatus*

*The precision electronic harmonium for studies into harmony and melody*

Leon Thérémin is playing Rachmaninov's Vocalise on his Théréminvox, Moscow Conservatoire, 1966

pen. "A pin would do," he decided bending over a length of film.

Soon the first track of synthetic sound was ready, the film threaded in the reproducer, and the machine started—the inventors smiled sadly. An ugly, grinding sound came out of the loudspeaker. It was a far cry from their elegant idea!

### ACOUSTICAL MONTAGE

Sholpo lived in Leningrad and Avraamov in Moscow. Soon they parted to begin independent work on synthetic music.

At Shorin's laboratory Sholpo found all that he needed to make a start: a place to work, a microscope to view and draw his sound curves and a machine to cut and splice films. Shorin advised him not to attempt to make new sound curves. As a beginning, he said, Sholpo should learn how to piece together simple tunes from prepared recordings of tones played on the flute and the clarinet. Sholpo did as he was told. Soon he had 'spliced' two songs, *Komarinskaya* and *Down the River Volga*. And not only the melodies. After a good deal of cutting and splicing, he was able to add a simple accompaniment.

This 'prefab' music soon interested the composer Georgy Rimsky-Korsakov, an enthusiast of all that was new in music. He asked Sholpo to 'splice' a few melodies for a short film, *The Year 1905 in Bourgeois Satire*. That was the beginning of the now much-talked-of 'acoustical montage'. It came just after the introduction of sound-on-film recording.

Sholpo did not linger for long copying known sounds. Nor did he think of processing them. He had a more ambitious goal—graphic or hand-drawn music.

Somehow or other he obtained a cartoon camera table—a fixture for making animated cartoons. He drew fancy curves on sheets of paper, photographed them on film on a reduced scale, developed the films, printed positives, passed them through a sound projector, and listened to the music. At first he did not care much about timbres or harmony. He just wanted to make melodies. And he did make them! Strange voices sang what the inventor had conceived—without pre-recorded music.

It was a terrible job, and proceeded at a snail's pace. On top of everything, he could not get rid of the annoying clicks at splices, however hard he tried. Soon Sholpo realized that if he was to get any further he needed a machine to draw sound curves. He thought of nothing else.

### THE VARIOPHONE

Sholpo pictured the machine in his mind like this: as in the Shorin sound recorder, a beam of light would write on a film; the film would move behind a slit; the vane rotating between the slit and the light source would change the slit's length.

Unlike the Shorin recorder, however, the vane, or acoustical drafter, as Sholpo called it, would be given a shape that would form the requisite serrations, that is, tones. The serrations could be made closer together or farther apart to give a higher or a lower pitch. The drafter's speed could be varied through a simple transmission—a pair of cones separated by a sphere. The film speed could be changed to vary the duration of the notes. After development and printing, the film could be played on an ordinary Shorin sound projector.

As you can see, the idea was not complicated, though not very simple either. It was far more difficult to get the money to build the machine, and to find a sound projector, at least an old one.

Sholpo took his hand-drawn melodies along to the Lenfilm Studios to play them and to ask for assistance.

"Hearty" is hardly the word for the reception he got there. "There's something in your idea," he was told, "but we can't take it at face value."

After a lot of questions and discussion, the film-makers made the inventor a shrewd offer; for four hundred roubles and an old sound projector he was to provide sound for one hundred metres of film in an animated cartoon using his new method. Should his work be turned down, he was to do it in the old way— with an orchestra—at his own expense. That would amount to thousands of roubles.

So the studio people safeguarded themselves against any failure, and the inventor faced a serious risk. But Sholpo signed the contract and got down to business. The four hundred he had been given was barely enough to buy the most essential materials and parts. As he said later, he built his machine with a pen-knife. But build it he did, the first machine to create synthetic music. It was made almost entirely of wood, and held together by string and wire.

Yet the machine, which the inventor called the Variophone, worked; the cones rotated, the film rustled by, and the light beam wrote music.

There was no time to make a test. Sholpo had to hurry to fulfil the contract. In ten days he had made music for two events in the film. The studio accepted his work without reservations. That was a victory.

**TOIL AND DEBATE**

The film *A Symphony of Peace* was conceived in 1933 as a lampoon on the hypocritical peace conferences that were going on in Europe at that time.

In the opening scene an orchestra of animals plays "peace music" under a tiger, the conductor. Then a soloist, another tiger, sings a barcarole. Next comes an inoffensive waltz suddenly interrupted by a burst of machine-gun fire from a hare's drum. After several scenes the musical instruments turn into rifles and guns, and a loud and shrill march can be heard, interrupted by shots. Finally, the music is drowned in the confused noises of the battlefield.

All the music and sound effects in the film came from the Variophone. *A Symphony of*

*Peace* was Sholpo's second film (unfortunately the film was not released because of some trouble with the colour).

Then followed other works. Graphic sound did well in the educational film *Carburation*. Gradually Sholpo gained experience for "big music".

In the mid-1930's the music enthusiasts in Moscow and Leningrad formed a society called the Autonomous Scientific-Technical Section, abbreviated to ANTES. The Moscow branch was headed by Boris Krasin, and the Leningrad branch by Rimsky-Korsakov, both active proponents of graphic music.

With ANTES's backing Sholpo built another Variophone, not so crude as its predecessor and more reliable and exact in operation.

Soon he was put at the head of a graphic sound laboratory at the Leningrad Institute of the Theatre and Music. True, the laboratory's staff consisted only of himself, and all the equipment he had was a table and two chairs. But he had more than enough enthusiasm for his work.

Synthetic music evoked interest. Its unusual quality made an impression, though sometimes it gave rise to heated debates. Some were enthusiastic about Sholpo's works, others were conservatively benevolent, while still others smiled and shrugged. Some criticized him severely for what they called mechanization of art. Sholpo fought back, putting all his vigour and conviction in his arguments: "If mechanization is not allowed, the only art that may exist is singing; we may only sing like birds.

As soon as man made a bow, stretched strings, and blew a pipe, he ushered in mechanization which has the right to develop indefinitely."

But Sholpo realized that deeds were better than words, however convincing. Only the sound of his music could win over supporters and defeat opponents. And the cones of the Variophone kept rotating; synthetic music came out in a continuous stream.

His incessant toil bore fruit. It was generally agreed that the Variophone could turn out passable light music like the artificial whistling in Robert's Song by Dunayevsky in the film *The Children of Captain Grant*. But the inventor was trying to create fresh beauty in the serious, classical repertoire. He 'drew' Liszt's *Sixth Rhapsody,* Chopin's *19th Prelude* and some works by Wagner, Bizet, Shostakovich and Prokofiev.

Graphic music was winning fame. And not only in Leningrad.

**OTHERS**

In the meantime Avraamov was active in Moscow, that same Avraamov who had come upon 'hand-drawn sound' with Sholpo. He set up a synthetic music laboratory at the Cine and Photo Research Institute.

It was Avraamov who made the world's first artificial sound recording on film in the summer of 1930. But he lacked Sholpo's inventive bent. The furthest he ventured was to photograph the sound curves he drew on paper with a cartoon camera table. As if to make up for this, he made a lot of use of synthetic sound to preserve folk music which did not fit into the traditional equal temperament of the piano. In fact, he saw the ultimate goal of synthetic music in the restoration of the natural musical scale.

He spent months in the villages of northern Russia, Kazakhstan, the Don valley, and the Caucasus, collecting folk airs. Using shorthand no one else could read, Avraamov jotted down marvellous melodies and tones which were beyond the reach of the usual musical notation. Back in Moscow, he transferred them onto film. In this he was helped by another admirer of the natural scale, the amateur composer Samoilov. Both are dead today.

Unfortunately during the war their records were lost in an absurd way. Someone liked the cans which held the films; he took the cans and threw away the films. Now we have only the word of Boris Yankovsky, who was another convinced supporter of synthetic music, and worked with Avraamov and Samoilov for some time. He speaks bitterly about the loss of the records.

Yankovsky took a different approach to synthetic music. This was fortunate. Sholpo, exuberant and dashing, did not trouble himself with "timbre-moulding", nor could his Variophone do much in that respect. Avraamov had no use at all for tone quality. His sound recordings were made of simple triangles which gave out rather colourless tones (he was mainly interested in melody). By contrast, Yankovsky attached equal importance to melody, harmony and tone quality. On top of that, he used mathematical analysis and built a synthesizer of his own design. True, it was just an improved cartoon camera table, and work on it was much slower than on the Variophone. But even so it produced unusual timbres.

Finally, leaving his "scientific" violins for the time being, (you read about it earlier in this book), Yankovsky moved to Leningrad, and joined Sholpo at his laboratory. Now both worked under the same roof, supporting each other and respecting each other's ideas.

### TRIUMPH

By 1940 Sholpo had done so much that was new and interesting that his superiors at the Institute of the Theatre and Music thought he deserved a master's degree in the history of art without a formal thesis. The papers they sent to the Higher Certification Commission (HCC) included praise from the leading composers Asafiev, Dzerzhinsky and Shostakovich, the scientists Andreyev and Frenkel, and Professor Struve, a prominent musicologist.

Soon the HCC summoned Sholpo. He went to Moscow, presented a short paper, demonstrated some of his graphic compositions, and left the stage to applause. The real surprise came later, when the HCC's decision was read. The inventor could not believe his ears. Instead of a master's degree, the Commission had conferred a doctorate upon him! That was a rare event in the HCC.

He came back home in high spirits. Everything was going well. The second Variophone was operating superbly. The quality of the phonograms he and Yankovsky were making began to improve considerably. The union of the two approaches promised to cure the "electric flavour" of synthetic music and give new effects. Great headway had been made on the theoretical side, especially on rhythm and its elusive nuances.

Then came an unexpected and terrible blow. War fell upon them like a bolt from the blue.

Yankovsky went to the front. The staff who had just learned to work as a team separated. Before long the front line ran through the suburbs of Leningrad. The ghastly months of the blockade began. But Sholpo kept working on synthetic music. He found a way of making his peaceful invention useful to the nation's war effort; the local Armed Forces Centre asked him to add sound to a propaganda cartoon, *The Vultures*, denouncing the Luftwaffe.

Sholpo got to work eagerly. Together with the composer Igor Boldyrev, he wrote the score and made phonograms quickly and well. His happy findings of timbres and succinct sound effects have retained their attraction till now.

The film begins with a parody of a march, boastful and insistent. As it plays, Hitler flings open a cage to let out his vulturous planes against the Soviet Union. Shepherd's horns, soft and sincere, stress the beauty of Russian landscape. The triumphant roar of engines rendered in bright, stylized tones and the cheerful *Air Force March* escort the Soviet fighters intercepting the enemy. Then comes the crash of shot-down Nazi planes. When their tails turn into cemetery crosses the sepulchral voices of the vanquished invaders can be heard, dreary and floating. Soon only carrion-crows pecking ominously at the crosses can be heard.

*The Vultures* was an immediate success with front-line units. Sholpo was happy and got ready for the next assignment. He asked for a sackful of oats as his fee for the film. This was a fortune in a sieged city where famine took a toll of thousands of human lives.

But he was prevented from working on another film. An enemy shell hit the attic at the Textiles Institute where Sholpo kept his Variophone. The valuable apparatus was smashed to pieces. As Boldyrev learned later, it was the last shell the Nazis fired at Leningrad.

Then followed several years of work at the Conservatoire in Tashkent where Sholpo was moved after Leningrad's blockade was broken through. After the war a period of the inventor's life began which was to end in tragedy.

**MURDER BY PROXY**

Now, after fifteen years, it is difficult to explain the failures that dogged the inventor who had become the head of a large graphic-sound laboratory since the end of the war. He had got all that he needed—a large staff, money and equipment. He had the rich experience of an inventor and he had authority. Yet work was not getting on well.

There seemed to be no end to their work on the third Variophone; there was always something to be altered or added. The laboratory was heavily in arrears; expenditure had mounted to one hundred thousand roubles, but the quality of their production remained hopelessly poor.

Could it be that Sholpo was a poor executive? Probably. A talented inventor and a forward-looking musician, he lacked managerial grasp. He was an enthusiast himself, and expected everybody around him to be one too. But that was not so. Yankovsky was away; Krasin was dead; ANTES no longer existed. Time and work dragged on bleakly. There was no inspiration to give energy. The thirst for anything new had given way to office routine. Sholpo realized that, but did not know what to do. He had allowed red tape to get hold of him; he felt it and was afraid—but saw no way out. Could it be age, the war, and fatigue? Probably.

In the meantime things at the laboratory took a turn for the worse. Then a newspaper lashed out at him. A good deal in its account was true. But a lot was missing: his youthful dream of a mechanical orchestra, the decades of unending work, the blockade months he had spent at his Variophone, *The Vultures* and the sackful of oats, the tragedy of an inventor who had failed to become an efficient manager.

The effect was quick. Sholpo had to visit the Public Attorney's office. There it was found out that he had done nothing criminal. Yet damage to his prestige as the head of the laboratory was irreparable. His former supporters now met him with pursed lips.

Soon his case was investigated by a fact-finding commission. The commission was reasonable and just. It was decided to integrate the laboratory with the Sound Recording Institute in Moscow. Sholpo was appointed a rank-and-file research worker. With his home in Leningrad, Sholpo could only come there now and then. Yet he was happy—his idea continued.

They began making a fourth Variophone at the Institute. This time it was planned to use magnetic tape instead of cine film, which was a major advance. You can easily imagine Sholpo's high hopes. They might have come true if it had not been for another "but".

Today you can't possibly say why it happened. It might have been the same killing indifference or lack of engineering experience. One way or another, though, after they had spent over four hundred thousand roubles, the designers at the Institute were unable to overcome the main drawback of the machine—the wow and flutter. The machine refused to sing, it only howled.

That was like the last straw which broke the camel's back. Back home at the end of 1950 Sholpo, exhausted by his worries, succumbed to cancer. A month later, early in 1951, he died.

CHAPTER TEN

*

# The Composer as a Painter

Dr. Sholpo's idea did not die with him. A man takes to his grave only what is his alone. What he has created for mankind remains alive and develops in spite of all that is transitory, accidental or hindering.

In the post-war years synthetic music took root at many motion picture and sound studios and spurred the invention of a great deal of apparatus. Although on a different basis and in other forms, the instruments of the Cologne Studio, Pierre Schaeffer's Phonogène, Myron Schaeffer's Hamograph and others are carrying on the principles which underlay Sholpo's work.

Not that these later workers borrowed their ideas directly from Sholpo. Yet it's gratifying for an admirer of Sholpo to learn that Olson, a leading U.S. acoustician, has built a computer-controlled music synthesizer using electric tuning-forks. The 'mechanical orchestra' in Sholpo's *The Enemy of Music* also uses them. But let us go back to what happened after Sholpo's death in his own country.

## IN THE SCRIABIN MUSEUM

It was in Moscow in 1960. I walked down Arbat Street, turned right at the Vakhtangov Theatre, and stopped in front of No. 11. The sign read: The Scriabin Museum. Closed on Wednesdays. The day was Wednesday, but muffled music was coming out of the first-floor windows.

I went up to the door and pressed the bell. The curator of the museum led me through the great composer's modest flat. I walked through the drawing-room, the dining-room, saw the black polish of two grands, and opened one more door when a powerful chord caught me unawares. It was a waterfall of music unlike anything I had ever heard before. Words are inadequate to describe its striking beauty. It was swelling, filling the air, gaining in strength; then—in an instant—it changed. The chords were now light, sparkling and dying away. Before I knew it, a peal of sound rang out, spreading round in a thousand fragments.

Silence fell. I looked around. The room was large. Unfinished displays stood at the walls. On one of them I read Scriabin's words from his programme to the *Fourth Sonata*, written in charcoal: "As fast as light, straight to the Sun, into the Sun".

Then I saw several tape recorders and loudspeakers, and two men by what looked like a printing press in a corner. That was where the music had come from—the music synthesizer developed by the inventor Yevgeny Murzin after many years of trial and error.

## FROM ELLINGTON TO SCRIABIN

Murzin was still a young student at the Civil Engineering College when Sholpo was climbing the ladder to triumph. He was equally good at his studies and invention. He invented a thousand and one things: hydraulic valves, charged-particle accelerators, brain-wave amplifiers. True, very few of his inventions were put into practice, but Murzin did not lose heart. He was twenty, and he had his studies, friends and music. Yes, music. It so happened that in the field of music his inventive genius was especially bright.

Like a good many young men, Murzin was a jazz enthusiast. He was fond of its beat, swing, and melody. He was ready and willing to dig deep into his pocket to collect recordings of the genuine originators of this folk art. And so he came upon Duke Ellington's records.

During one of his visits to a record shop he was listening to a new recording by Ellington when another customer looked at him inquisitively and asked:

"Do you really like it?"

"I certainly do."

They got into conversation. Murzin learned from his new acquaintance that a lot of Ellington's recordings were head arrangements never committed to paper. What his band usually played for a recording session was collective improvisation.

At the end of their long talk the man said in a friendly tone, "I think you're ready for serious music. Take my word, before long Scriabin will be your favourite."

That was the beginning of the long friendship between Murzin and Konstantin Soloshek, then an employee at the Radio Committee's recording archives and now the manager of a record shop in Moscow.

Soloshek proved right. Before long, Murzin added recordings of Rachmaninov, Liszt, Bach, Wagner, Musorgsky and, finally, Scriabin, to his collection.

### THE ORIGIN OF AN IDEA

His discovery of Scriabin astounded Murzin. Nothing had ever affected him so deeply before. Murzin revelled in Scriabin's command of music, tone colours and patterns of harmony. The passion of youth is like a spring thunderstorm —light, invigorating and gay. He read everything that he could find about Scriabin. Then he delved deeply into musical acoustics. Natural intervals, overtones, and temperament all became his household words. He felt keenly the composer's desire to overcome the limitations of the traditional musical scale. But how could it be done?

He thought for a long time and suddenly had a promising idea. He imagined a machine which would produce any musical sounds, intervals and timbres—everything—to the composer's liking. Or would it? He could not believe his luck.

It took Soloshek some time to understand the inventor's idea. When he did, he could hardly keep quiet:

"Now, my boy, there is no time to be lost.

Go straight to the acoustics laboratory at the Conservatoire."

And Murzin went. Nervous and confused, he told Professor Garbuzov, who headed the laboratory at that time, about his idea.

"The idea of synthetic music is not new, young man. Sholpo is working on it in Leningrad, and Avraamov and Yankovsky in Moscow. You'd better go to Yankovsky," the professor told him quietly.

His first meeting with Yankovsky was both happy and sad. Murzin met an enthusiast who shared his conviction, but who also realized how difficult it would be to build his apparatus. Synthetic music was still in its infancy; it lacked financial support and facilities. It would be naive to expect anyone to build an experimental model of Murzin's machine, which would be far more complex and expensive than cartoon camera tables or even the Variophone. The invention was not a priority. It promised no economic return. As to its aesthetic value—well, that could not be proved with drawings, Yankovsky told him.

Murzin listened to all that the other man had to say. Then both sat down to analyze the idea in detail. Yankovsky liked the principle of music synthesis. Murzin was given a good deal of expert advice and came to believe in his project—unexpectedly tricky and nearly unfeasible, and therefore all the more alluring.

"Why," Murzin said to himself, "I have the whole of my life before me, I can build the machine with my own hands, in my own good time."

But he had to postpone his project. And for a long time too. The year 1941 came, and with it—war.

### THE GOAL

It was not until after the war that Murzin, now an experienced military instrumentation engineer, could find time for his pet project that he had never forgotten since his student days.

In 1947 Soloshek came back from the army, and they met again. Gradually a group of music enthusiasts gathered around them, giving much-needed support at a difficult time. Only Yankovsky was still away. Murzin tried to trace him but couldn't.

Time went by. Finally they assembled two tape recorders, a hundred-valve amplifier, and an electric drive. While on a business trip to East Germany, Murzin ordered optical parts of top-quality glass. They were made by the famous Zeiss Werke. In Moscow he got a framework for his machine.

A good many people helped the inventor unselfishly. His superiors also gave him useful assistance. His workmates—fitters, mechanics and opticians—took a hand in many parts. The designers advised on the general layout of the components.

The project progressed. But not always smoothly.

His life brought him both happiness and mirth. He had a goal to achieve and work to carry on. In the daytime, at his office, he was busy investigating tricky instrumentation schemes and experimenting for his master's degree; in the evenings, back in his country house, he had his project now so painfully dear to him. The days were crowded. Sometimes, however, oppressive fatigue would overcome him and he would see no escape from bitterness after failures.

And the failures were many, especially when he was making glass disks for his machine. There were to be four identical disks covered with a precise pattern of one hundred and fifty concentric rings varying regularly in opacity. A displacement of a few hundredths of a millimetre would be intolerable, as would the smallest irregularity in opacity. Murzin decided to draw the pattern photographically on plates and devised a fixture to speed up the operation.

More often than not he would sit up well into the small hours with his tired eyes glued to the voltmeter, the disk rotating, and his hand turning the rheostat knob by habit. Then a lamp would blow unexpectedly and twenty hours' work would come to nothing.

It took him fifty hours of close work and adjustment to draw a pattern on a disk. It involved about two thousand operations of high precision.

Murzin and his wife took turns working at the drawing fixture. Their motto now was "Draw or die!" They would hastily instruct any guest who turned up at their house and seat him or her at the apparatus. It was more fun than work, and that was the way they did it—day after day and night after night.

Troubles awaited them at every step. Sometimes the local station would stop the supply of electricity, and they would have to change over to storage batteries. The batteries would run down before they had completed the pattern, and the disk would have to be rejected. There were rejects because of a broken pin, a miscount, poor emulsion, or just a drop in temperature outdoors and, as a result, wrong development.

Over three years were spent making the only disk—the negative for the four positives needed in the machine. At last it was complete, a thin, circular plate of glass covered with an odd pattern. Looking at it, Murzin thought it would have been far simpler to do the job at a factory, on a precision machine-tool.

**FROM THE BARREL ORGAN TO THE MUSIC SYNTHESIZER**

The first prototype of the machine (or mock-up, as Murzin called it) was put together by 1957. It occupied half a room in the inventor's country house. It looked unsightly, showing bare parts, entangled wires and rows of valves. Yet it bore the name of photo-electronic optical sound synthesizer, as Murzin called it in the patent he eventually took out. The main thing was that the machine worked.

To get an idea of how it worked, let's look at mechanical musical instruments.

The earliest of them were musical boxes and barrel organs. They were simple: a clock spring rotated a cylinder studded with pins or pegs which either struck strips of metal graduated to produce different tones or plucked strings.

Then there were the piano player and the automatic piano. These could change their repertoire and play different music. The piano player had a row of pins linked to hammers. The pins were held against a perforated paper roll which moved across the pins. As it moved, the perforations also moved. When a perforation came over a pin, the pin actuated the hammer linked to it, and the hammer struck a string. The other pins and hammers worked the same way. In fact, the perforated paper roll was the score. A composer could "write" it with a pair of scissors, and it would then be played without a human performer.

Some of the automatic pianos were very good. They could convey all the finest nuances of a performance. They could also "memorize" a pianist's playing. After a pianist had played his piece the piano could reproduce it so faithfully that you would not be able to tell it from the "live" performance. Today such instruments have been made obsolete by sound recording. But they suggested to Sholpo his idea of the mechanical orchestra in his story, *The Enemy of Music*.

His story, too, features a moving, perforated strip. It is a very wide strip, extending from wall to wall. It is black, and impenetrable to light. But why is it black? Because in this machine instead of pins the inventor uses beams of light passing through the perforations in the strip and falling on photoresistors wound with selenium wire. When light falls on a photoresistor, its resistance drops and a current begins to flow from a cell to an electric tuning-fork and a horn resonator (invented way back by Helmholtz). The machine has hundreds of tuning-forks, all producing pure tones which can be blended to give fantastic timbres.

Now it's not difficult to grasp the way Murzin's machine operates. It, too, has photo-cells, a moving black disk with transparent strips, and beams of light. It has no tuning-forks, though. Instead, tones are produced in a more ingenious way. In effect, the principle on which it operates is altogether different. But let's begin at the beginning.

**LIGHT AND SOUND**

Imagine yourself sitting at a desk. Running across its width on the opposite side is a horizontal slit. In the slit you can see flashes of light. If you look more closely you will notice that the slit is made up of a multitude of steps, or chromas. There is a total of 576 chromas. In the one furthest to the left the light goes on and off forty times a second. As you move to the right, the flickers become faster. In the right-hand chroma, the frequency is 11,000 per second. The frequency increases by the same amount with each step.

Of course, you can't see the flickering—it is too fast for that. It is produced by intercepting the light beams on their way to the chromas, using revolving disks with an undulating pattern, the very disks which were so hard to make.

Now the slit is the very basis of Murzin's synthesizer. It silently stocks any tone required, for flickers can be made to sound. Just place photo-cells in front of the slit, connect them to a good amplifier and loudspeaker, and the variations of light will be turned into sound waves. True, all the chromas will sound at once, which will make a dreadful noise, while we need musical sounds. But they can be picked out from the noise quite simply.

Put an opaque plate with a hole over the slit. Let the hole be over the chroma where light flickers 440 times a second. Now only these variations of light will be allowed to reach the amplifier. When converted to sound waves they will produce a very pure middle A.

You don't like the tone, do you? It's too dull, you say? Well, it can easily be remedied. Prick a few more holes in the plate so that they open other places in the slit, corresponding to the higher harmonics of middle A. Now the tone is rich and bright. It's a truly musical sound. And you've got it in the most efficient way—by blending pure overtones.

Several sets of such holes in the plate will produce a chord. It can be as complex as required, with any number of notes. The notes can be arranged in the traditional chromatic scale of equal temperament (as in the grand piano, the organ, or the accordion), or they can be spaced at truly perfect intervals, which are inaccessible to most instruments and existing musical notation.

The point is that Murzin's machine uses a scale which is more complex than the ordinary chromatic scale. Instead of twelve notes to an octave it has seventy-two, or six times as many. The synthesizer can give very slight changes in the pitch of a tone, hardly discernible by the most sensitive ear. All this has been done so as to approach a continuous scale in which every interval can be made perfect—as with the unaccompanied violin of today.

The seventy-two notes to an octave had been suggested by Yankovsky before the war. According to him, a 72-note scale could give especially bright timbres and sonorous concords.

In principle, Murzin's machine is capable of all that Sholpo dreamed of: any concords, rich timbres, any harmonic patterns, a multitude of perfect consonances, and unheard-of disonances. Because of this, Murzin thought it appropriate to call his brainchild 'ANS', after his favourite composer Alexander Nikolayevich Scriabin.

### THE 'PARTITURA' AND THE CODER

Music is made up of variations of tones in time, tempo, rhythm, melody, loudness and other effects. Murzin's machine can do all that. The plate covering the slit is not stationary; it can move like the paper roll in the automatic piano player. Instead of perforations it has transparent stripes.

The plate is made of glass and given a coat of opaque paint. Murzin has called it the 'partitura', or score, which is what composers call a copy of a composition. But while an ordinary score is silent without an orchestra, the partitura in Murzin's machine can do perfectly well without one. It's a "self-playing" score.

You remove paint from the plate with a stylus to produce transparent stripes, switch on the motor, and the partitura moves between the slit and the photo-cells. As it moves it uncovers the various chromes to the photo-cells. The flickers of various frequencies combine to produce notes. They vary, change into other notes, die out and rise again—exactly as "ordered" by the transparent stripes cut on the partitura.

As a matter of fact, anything can be cut on the partitura—the tones of the violin, piano, trumpet, orchestra and even the human voice, if you please. You only need to know the harmonic content of the tones, their attack and the way they decay. You can produce timbres and harmonic patterns which are beyond the reach of any electrophonic instruments, and the sounds of a waterfall, hammer or thunder. But again you must know everything about these sounds, which is where the main difficulty lies. It will take years to break the code of the world of sound.

Not that there is nothing to go by—the inventor has laid down the basic rules, an ABC, for using his synthesizer and the partitura. He has added a coder to make composition-writing easier.

The coder looks like this. A picture of the piano keyboard is fitted above the partitura giving the "reference points" of the 12-note chromatic scale. Another scale on a carriage alongside the keyboard gives the positions of the first sixteen partials for any fundamental tone. With this arrangement you can conveniently produce exact partials and perfect intervals for any note. The desired tone quality can be obtained with fine styli fixed at the requisite points on the carriage. The styli have round knobs of different colours. ("The composer should have something round to hold," Murzin says.)

The coder looks like an improved drafting machine, and work on it resembles that of a draftsman, except that the composer uses the black plate of the partitura instead of a sheet of drawing paper.

### THE START OF A SUCCESSFUL CAREER

In 1957 the machine did not yet have the convenient coder, and it was not easy to "cut" sounds. But Murzin was impatient to show his ANS to people versed in music. What would composers say? What would Yankovsky say? And he set out to search for his first adviser again. This time he found Yankovsky at the Experimental Music Factory in Moscow.

Yankovsky went to Murzin's country house with Boldyrev, the composer who had been an assistant to Sholpo. Yankovsky spent several hours at the synthesizer and found it satisfactory. In fact, he had not expected such a result, he said. He gave the inventor a lot of advice, but on how to improve a good thing and not how to save a poor one. That much was clear to Murzin.

Boldyrev compared the synthesizer with the Variophone and found it superior to Sholpo's invention in many respects.

Soon the composer Andrei Volkonsky came to see the invention. After he had learned what was what in the machine, he set down at the partitura to "cut" sounds and made a discovery quite unexpected even by the inventor himself. Instead of narrow stripes Volkonsky had cut broad bands covering several chromas at a time at the bass end of the partitura. What they then heard were the powerful bass tones of an organ, only brighter and more sonorous.

"That's the thing for me," Volkonsky said.

Simonov and Korsunsky, the makers of electrophonic instruments, and Rudakov of the Acoustics Laboratory at the Moscow Conservatoire were equally enthusiastic about Murzin's invention.

In the autumn of 1959 the synthesizer was given its finishing touches and taken to Moscow where it found a hospitable shelter at the Scriabin Museum. There it was put to work by Murzin and Nikolai Nikolsky, a composer, musician and radio engineer. Before long they composed *The Russian Fantasia*, a chaste and quiet piece, and a charming and wonderfully unpredictable miniature. Then Pyotr Meshchaninov, a young composer, joined them. Besides writing music they were working on a new theory of harmony which would take music beyond the old 12-note equal-tempered scale.

To their delight quite a number of composers visited the museum to hear the synthesizer and left warm and encouraging notes in the Visitors' Book.

"The ANS is undoubtedly of great interest to composers. It will stimulate their imagination and creativity," wrote Dmitry Shostakovich.

"It may well happen that the ANS will open up an entirely new world of sounds, tone colours, modes, rhythms and harmonies never heard before and therefore identifiable with other galaxies, space flight, green and crimson suns, and living creatures never seen anywhere. It embodies both similarity and difference. In this lie astounding possibilities for the sounds of our world to be interpreted in a new manner," wrote Mikhail Chulaki.

"It's a remarkable machine. I'm all in favour of this wonderful invention being used by every musician," Nikita Bogoslovsky added briefly.

"The ANS is an outstanding development which may have far-reaching consequences. For the first time in the history of musical art music-writing and music-playing have been united. Now the composer and the performer may be a single person. If properly used, the ANS may prove a revolutionary invention befitting this age of sputniks and space travel," Andrei Volkonsky wrote.

Finally, here is the opinion of Nikolai Andreyev, a scientist who has devoted all his life to acoustics:

"What I have seen and heard at Murzin's has deeply impressed me. Using his apparatus, which in my opinion is almost perfect, the composer can work on an entirely different basis. I am familiar with the previous attempts made here in the Soviet Union. I also know the similar instrument built by Olson in the United States. I believe Murzin has gone one better them all."

#### THE COMPOSER AS A PAINTER

When an artist is painting, he dabs his canvas, steps back to look at the picture, and then changes or adds something. He can always see what he is creating. The same is true of sculptors, writers and poets.

But a symphonic composer usually cannot do so. He has to rely on a good deal of intuition and imagination which can be tested only when an orchestra performs his composition.

The situation is different with Murzin's synthesizer. However complex, the composition can be heard, improved and enlarged as soon as it has been written. After a part of the composition has been completed on the partitura, it can be recorded on tape. During a tape-recording session the composer can go on creating music. Now he is a conductor, varying the tempo, rhythm, intensity, attack and decay of his music as he pleases. The synthesizer has controls for all of these effects.

This is a major advantage over Sholpo's graphic music where composition and reproduction were separated by a lengthy and troublesome procedure of developing and drying the film, making, developing and again drying a positive.

Murzin's machine also compares favourably with some of the foreign synthesizers, such as

Olson's apparatus which uses a perforated paper strip. In fact, the composer only writes a programme for the Olson synthesizer, and the music is synthesized by laboratory technicians. The Olson machine can only write two-part music. Multi-part compositions entail superimposing parts repeatedly.

Needless to say, Murzin's synthesizer outclasses any sound-recording equipment with its sound processing, montage, mixing and reverberations.

The ANS is an instrument for the composer. It needs no intermediaries. It provides a direct link between visual and musical perception. Music comes from lines drawn by the human hand.

### A PROGRAMME OF WORK

When the second Russian edition of this book was going to press, Murzin had completed a new model of the ANS. It has a compass of ten octaves giving a total of 720 notes, a high-quality amplifier, an eight-channel recording system so that eight-part music can be recorded, and a cluster of power speakers made especially for Murzin by the Radio and Acoustics Institute.

In fact the new ANS is no longer just a synthesizer; it can play its own music. It is an excellent instrument with a compass of 720 tones!

Of course, one man cannot play this giant. He would need sixty fingers. It can be played by six performers—a sort of electronic sextet.

There are six keyboards on separate consoles. Each looks like the keyboard of a piano, only a little wider. Any pianist can play it without having to learn anew. But the six keyboards are tuned differently; each is shifted one chroma, or one-sixth of a semitone, with respect to the next. As a result, the six keyboards cover all of the 720 tones continuously.

For the composer's convenience Murzin has invented a simple but ingenious notation covering the ANS's range. The performers need not know it; their parts bear no new symbols.

And so Handel's old dream has come true; an instrument has been built, free from the limitations imposed by Werckmeister's clever but rigid system—12-note equal temperament. The ANS uses a 72-note equally-tempered scale.

Now music has a machine which can imitate any instrument, a whole orchestra and the human voice. Are the violin and piano no longer needed? Can we do without Carusos and Chaliapins? Is it worth while training them now that "synthetic singing" can so easily be prepared?

"Nonsense. The ANS is not an ape," Murzin protests.

He is not a megalomaniac. He agrees that the ANS could imitate the piano, the violin or the voice. It would be feasible, although incredibly difficult. But it would be sensible only as part of research and not as a new art. Genuine art has never risen out of imitation. The human voice will always be of aesthetic value as such, and so will the piano. The symphony orchestra cannot be imitated. Nor will the miraculous violin crying in the hands of a human performer ever die.

The ANS is no enemy of present-day music; it threatens nothing, Murzin says. He is looking forward to the time when enthusiasts and lovers of any music—symphonic or jazz—will use his synthesizer, for its only purpose is to roll back the frontiers of musical art.

That is the reason why the inventor has come out with a somewhat controversial statement: the ANS must not be used for classical music. Bach, Tchaikovsky and Scriabin wrote for the organ, the violin, the piano and the drum, Murzin says. Playing their music on a new scale and in new tone colours would be the same as copying Rembrandt and Repin with different paints.

It remains to be seen whether or not Murzin is right. He does not hold that his view is immutable; there may be exceptions, such as works lending themselves readily to the natural scale, like Scriabin's music. In any case the ANS must preserve its originality.

CHAPTER ELEVEN

\*

# Music from the Computer

In this age of nuclear power and space travel man is not easily surprized. He takes for granted the vacuum cleaner and television, supersonic airliners and chess-playing machines. The fantasy of yesterday is commonplace today; fairy tales are coming true. Against the background of such great advances in science, the contributions that physics is making to music appear simple and natural.

Yet in recent years developments have taken musicians unawares. Word went round about machines which could write music, electronic contraptions which were expected to mechanize the very basis of all art—human inspiration.

Electronic composers receive a good deal of publicity today, especially when the unlimited potentialities of computers are being demonstrated. Things that nobody would believe some twenty years ago are today giving rise to increasingly bold ideas and projects, disputes and arguments.

What is actually there behind this surprise? What is the music-writing computer like? Where does its creative inspiration come from? Is it as amazing as it is said to be?

#### MOZART'S TABLES

Some two hundred years ago many people in Europe liked to amuse themselves with 'music tables'. The great Mozart wrote a jocular book, *The Manual for Writing Waltzes by Means of Dice without Any Knowledge of Music and Composition.*

That book saved all the trouble. All a would-be composer needed were a pair of dice, music paper, ink and a quill pen. He threw the dice, counted them, looked up the dice count in the first column of the "Table of Numbers" to get the number of the respective square in the "Table of Music" and copied the first bar of a waltz given there in musical notation. He got all the eight bars of the first movement of a waltz in the same way. Then followed another eight throws of dice, and the second movement of a waltz was composed with the aid of the second column in the "Table of Numbers". There were no "throes of creation" to suffer from.

What was then left for the "composer" to do was to sign the composition, roll the paper, put a silk band on the roll, and offer it as a present to his lady so that on playing the piece, she could say, "Oh, darling, you're just as good as Mozart himself!" And it would be no exaggeration.

It would not be at all difficult to mechanize Mozart's tables. Any watchmaker could build a clockwork device which would throw dice, draw plates with music symbols, and piece them together into bars of a waltz like building a house from toy bricks.

In fact, many of the much-talked-of electronic composers work on a very similar principle.

### MACHINE INSPIRATION

It is true that the electronic composer uses no bricks. Nor does it know music notation. It handles only figures. Therefore music has first to be translated into a language of digits, and bars or even whole pieces of music fed into the machine's memory as groups of numbers. In order to do this the numbers are punched on a paper or plastic strip which, as it unfolds, causes suitable signals to be sent to the computer's memory. In the same way the machine is given instructions for combining and arranging the number groups. That's all there is to it.

Then you press the start button on the control console, and the computer sets to work "creating" music. It re-combines and re-arranges the groups of numbers in a multitude of ways, exactly as instructed. Beams of electrons shoot in the valves, the neon lamps flash, and in a few seconds the "composition" is finished. The computer reads it out as a column of figures on a paper strip. Finally, the figures are translated back into musical language. In this way

Pinkerton in the United States has obtained a multitude of combinations from the bits of thirty-nine pop songs. Brooks, Hopkins, Neuman and Wright, also in the United States, have similarly processed thirty-seven hymns of different races from different times.

In fact, these experiments differ but little from Mozart's "table compositions". The only difference is that the computer does the job at an incredibly high rate, thousands of songs an hour!

### A SYMPHONY IN BLOTS

According to Ma Su-chien, an historian, dice were widely used by composers way back in ancient China. In any case, they figured at the examinations of young composers.

An examinee would throw dice several times in succession and memorize the count. Each number stood for a note, and their combination for a series of notes. Now this accidental chain of notes had to be processed according to the rules of music so as to obtain a fairly pleasant tune. A similar procedure is still used at some conservatoires to test students' ability to compose.

Another method of music-writing was suggested by the English composer Hayes in a satirical book he wrote in 1751. His "exceptionally new method" consisted in making ink stains on music paper with a shoe-brush.

Carrying his joke a step farther in the manner of Chinese "dice composition", we can get a very close analogy to another method of computer music-writing.

Suppose a composer is brimful of ideas but has only a sheet of music paper covered with blots strewn at random, some white paint and no ink. The situation is absurd, but what he can do?

Well, there is a way out. Instead of placing notes on the stave, he can remove surplus blots by covering them up with the white paint.

There are blots all over the paper, on and between the lines. There are 'C' blots, and 'A' blots, and blots for all the other notes. Some are bigger and can be taken for whole notes, or semibraves. Others are smaller and can well stand for half notes, or minims. Still smaller blots will do as quarter notes, or crotchets, eighth notes, or quavers, and so on.

Our composer patiently weeds the crop of blots, leaving only those he wants to remain in his music.

The same sort of job can be done by the computer. And it will no longer be making primitive rearrangements of existent bits of music. The music will be composed anew and not cribbed.

### AN ELECTRONIC PALESTRINA

The electronic weeding of a blotted sheet of music paper is far more difficult than piecing together bits of existent music to give new tunes. Of course, there is neither a brush, nor white paint, nor ink. Everything is translated into mathematical language as before. But instead of bits of music, a digital analogue of random blots—"noise"—is fed into the computer's memory. This is a chaos of numbers in no way related to one another. At the same time the computer is instructed how to "weed" the digital "noise" mathematically. The instructions are now more complicated—they should measure up to the knowledge and intuition of our hypothetical composer painting over blots on the stave.

This, as you can see, is a tougher job, but again there is nothing supernatural about it. In fact, what we have is the familiar 'selection from noise' only in another guise. We saw it at work in Simonov's noisephone, the graphic-sound method, and Murzin's synthesizer. Although the instruments are different, the goal is the same, "Choose the best possible". Like buying a necktie at a shop. The better and fuller the instructions thought out by man, the better the music that the computer will write.

The first successful attempt at computer music was made by Hiller and Isaacson at the University of Illinois, who succeeded in programming the Illiac, a large digital computer, to produce original compositions. After a year's work, a students' amateur string quartet performed the experimental *Illiac Suite* composed by the computer.

The *Illiac Suite* consisted of four movements. Each movement had been composed by the computer to different rules. In the first, the machine had been given a limited freedom of choice. The numbers symbolizing the notes had been selected with all the rigidity of classical harmony. And the composition came out in a style favoured some three hundred years ago. Sound combinations had been selected and organized as they would have been by Giovani da Palestrina, the founder of the classical system. That was confirmed by the classical music experts present at the recital. Not that there was anything original about the piece. The computer had just done a simple exercise in harmonization, an exercise ordinary even by a music school's standards.

In the fourth movement the computer had been free to do almost anything. And the composition was very much like modern music—an encouraging result for Hiller and Isaacson.

So, when properly programmed by man, a computer can construct chords, piece together new songs from the bits of old ones, and even approach modern music. Is that all? Why so much enthusiasm? Can the computer create anything of practical value?

### ZARIPOV'S IDEA

Rudolph Zaripov, a Soviet mathematician, first started thinking about computer music in 1947, when he still lived in his native city of Kazan and was going to a music school.

He was a devoted amateur mathematician and noticed that the school's harmonization of melodies could be conveniently formulated mathematically. He tried several methods of calculating chords and found the job could be done by any calculator. And immediately he thought of computing not only chords but also melody, the main component of music. For melody must certainly be governed by laws, he reasoned, and the laws can be given mathematical form.

But he could not make a dent in the formidable problem of the mathematical formalization and calculation of melody. The task proved too big for him. Nor could he find so much as a trace of a hint in books. The young man's quest remained unanswered.

Out of the musical school and sticking to his favourite, the cello, Zaripov went to university. Later he added drawing to music and mathematics, and finally he joined the ranks of shortwave radio hams. That quiet, inconspicuous young man had enough energy for many widely differing interests. He was always eager to do something else, to kill several birds with one stone. And, contrary to the old saying, he never missed one.

After he enrolled as a post-graduate at Rostov University, his old idea of a musical computer became one such bird and took control of him finally when, as a master of science, he went to Moscow to learn the operation of the Urals computer.

He knew nothing about the experiments with computer music carried on in the United States. Probably, that was to his advantage. Zaripov went his own way to train the computer to compose melodies.

At the dead of night in July, 1959, you could see a light on in a solitary window on the thirteenth floor of Moscow University's hostel on the Lenin Hills. That was the small room where Zaripov sat up over endless computations. At dawn he went to bed for an hour or two, and at eight in the morning he walked to one of Moscow's research establishments to practise on the computer. All day long he ran the machine solving knotty mathematical problems. In the evening, after everyone else had gone, he stayed at the controls to "train" the computer—with the permission of Boris Romanov, its chief—to compose music. At night he again prepared programmes for the next day.

He worked as if in a daze, at the limit of his power, without so much as a minute's break and eating very little. He couldn't do it any other way, he thought, with so little time left.

At first his progress was slow. The Urals proved a complete failure in its first trials—it could "think up" nothing sensible. That was because the subtle, sometimes subconscious melodic patterns escaped mathematical formalization. Zaripov analyzed a multitude of compositions only to discover an endless variety of melodic patterns. The laws of melody proved far more complicated and less studied than those of harmony.

Yet, step by step, he was making headway. Sometimes he would do what had already been done—by musicologists, not computer engineers. Later, for example, he discovered *On Melody*, a book by Professor Masel of the Moscow Conservatoire, and found in it a wealth of knowledge about melodic forms. But at the time, in 1959, he did not know the book. Instead, he had to programme the computer from scratch.

Finally Zaripov came to terms with the computer. Any note was to be specified by a five-digit number, the first two digits giving the ordinal number of the note, the third its duration, and the remaining two its pitch. Any melody was always to end with the tonic or key-note. The progress towards the final note should always be in as short intervals as possible. There should be not more than six notes in a series, either ascending or descending. Adjacent intervals adding to more than an octave were vetoed. There were also other rules for changing the direction of melody.

A separate section of the programme was devoted to time signatures: four-beat times for marches, triple times for waltzes, and so on. Care was also taken of the number of bars in a movement and movements in a composition.

### 'THE URALS TUNES'

At long last it was ready, the first algorithm—a set of mathematical rules for composing melodies. The first programme based on it was written for the computer, punched on tape and fed into the computer's memory. Zaripov adjusted the 'random number generator', the source of 'digital noise' from which the Urals was to pick its melodies, and pressed the start button. The machine was supposed to compose a waltz. In a few seconds it was ready—printed on a paper strip. The button was pressed again, and a second waltz came out. Zaripov did not know yet what sort of music it was. He would decipher the numbers later, at night. And now he ordered a march.

This time, however, something inexplicable happened. For some reason the Urals refused to compose a march. It revolted, stopped of its own accord, then started up the programme strip and kept running it. The huge electronic machine, occupying several rooms, was foolishly twinkling its neon eyes without turning out a single bit of music.

Zaripov stopped the machine and ordered one more waltz. Everything was fine again—in a few seconds he had in his hands another roll with a waltz encoded in columns of five-digit numbers. When he tried to order a march again, the Urals threw another fit.

"Well, of all the silly ..." he muttered. "Why should this damn thing hate marches?"

It was only the day before he was to leave Moscow that the cause of the trouble was detected. It turned out that Zaripov had written '1177' instead of '1777' in the programme. This had sent the computer on a false track.

The last evening the Urals composed only marches.

Zaripov could only sit down to decode the computer's compositions when he was back at home, in Rostov. Some of them were not too bad. Of course, none could compete with *Mos-*

*cow Nights*. But, he thought, they were after all only the first computer compositions.

A year later *The Papers of the U.S.S.R. Academy of Sciences* carried Zaripov's publication, "On the Algorithmic Description of Music Writing". It had been sponsored by Sobolev, a leading Soviet mathematician. It was probably the first time that the most venerable of all Russian scientific journals had published a piece of music. This music had been born from knowledge put into a machine and not from human inspiration. Later in the popular science magazine, *Knowledge Is Power*, Zaripov called his music *The Urals Tunes*.

### USES FOR THE ROBOT COMPOSER

Now we've learned enough to feel greater respect for the robot composer. It knows not only how to take and use other composers' music but also how to form and relate chords into passable tunes.

"If so, can't the robot composer do the work of the human composer?" a captious reader might ask.

Well, it depends on what human composer. It can replace a mediocre one at once if you like. And probably with advantage. Good music from the computer, on the other hand, is still far off. Probably in the remote future, after a good deal of research, man will learn how to instruct the computer to organize music in the same way as Palestrina or Bach or Mozart.

Even today some engineers (not musicians!)

are thinking of making the computer translate a literary work into 'musical language'. For example, the computer could find the 'literary algorithm' for Pushkin and the 'musical algorithm' for Tchaikovsky, correlate them and turn the poem *Eugene Onegin* into an opera again. Imitating the famous composer, the computer would write melancholy music to pensive verses and gay passages to cheerful lines. Wishful thinking? Absurd? Well, you can never tell. In any case computer engineers are quite serious about it. Indeed they believe the computer could extend the creative life of composers. If Tchaikovsky had not completed *The Queen of Spades*, the machine could do that in Tchaikovsky's idiom, they say. Similarly, it could write new operas, concertos and symphonies to other poems and novels in the manner of Tchaikovsky.

There is no denying, their plan, if realized, would be a major achievement for science. Even limited success, a remote similarity between computer music and the man-composed work taken as a standard, would prove that science has at last got a deep insight into the creative system of the composer (incidentally, the algorithm for this could be formulated by the same computer). Still, this experiment, for all its complexity, would hardly be of any musical value.

The computer just cannot measure up to its creator for the simple reason that there is something inside man no computer, however perfect, will ever simulate. The computer is destined to remain inferior to man.

Whatever its "training", the computer just cannot create like a true artist. For man has feelings, which are denied to the most perfect robot. Only man can feel sorrow, happiness, love or hatred; only man, continually changing, can reflect in himself the continually changing world.

A genuine composer creates every new work in a new way and not to a hard and fast rule. His style and mood vary imperceptibly from work to work, from movement to movement, from bar to bar. Although they can be formalized mathematically, such changes cannot be computed in advance, because man draws them from the world, people and events around him. The greater a composer, the clearer the picture of the world he sees, and the more subtle and deeper the imprint he leaves on musical tradition.

Because of all this the machine will never take the place of the composer—the creative artist who knows the way to human hearts.

Yet the robot composer holds out great promise.

It would be tempting, for example, to "cross" the styles, even though simplified, of two different composers and to see what comes out. Or a composer's works can be tested for originality. Just feed his works into the computer and get an exhaustive answer like this one: "This composition is 50 per cent an imitation of composer A, 40 per cent an imitation of composer B, and only 10 per cent original." This would be quite useful, because there is no originality in many compositions.

Joking apart, the computer should become an excellent instrument for experiments with musical sounds, patterns, modes and scales. The composer could entrust complex harmonization to his robot and with its aid test newly invented musical structures. The computer may well speed up and facilitate work on musical synthesizers. Obedient and helpful, it will conduct the electronic orchestra, thus helping the composer to create extremely complex and long compositions much faster and easier than he can today.

CHAPTER TWELVE

*

# Physics and Music

In a good many science-fiction novels our descendants are pictured as living in an environment crowded with physics, electronics, cybernetics, ubiquitous machines and a multitude of robots of all descriptions and for any purpose—clever, efficient, passionless and dedicated. From the pages of space fiction strange nuclear-electronic musical systems beam at us and we read the gobbledygook names of cosmic symphonies, devastatingly imposing and deliberately obscure. This book, too, it would seem, points to the inevitable surrender of musical art to electrical engineering, mechanization and automation. One might well get scared!

Indeed, some fear that this technological avalanche rushing upon us will wipe out its creator—man—ousting him from the arts against his will. Although today the music created by man's brain, voice and hands still holds its ground firmly and more esoteric sources of music are still in embryo, will this remain so tomorrow? Will man, that sluggish, slow-thinking creature, be able to win the competition with his nimble brainchild?

It is an old problem—the relationship between man and machine. There has been a lot of hot talk about it. Since Mary Woolstonecraft's *Frankenstein* and Karel Čapek's remarkable play *R.U.R.* from which the very word 'robot' has come, many an author has prophesied a revolt of machines against man and man's destruction by robots. Norbert Wiener himself has warned us against this danger and advised us to take precautions in advance.

Most scientists do not see eye to eye with him, however. In their opinion, man has and can have nothing to fear about machines. He has always been and will remain the master, however clever they may be.

As to new sources of music, in the hands of intelligent and humane users who love life, have a feeling for the present and foresee the future, they will lead man to the ultimate command of the beautiful and boundless world of sound.

### YESTERDAY, TODAY AND TOMORROW

Today our life is richer in and fuller of music than it was yesterday, and much of this is due to progress in engineering. Tomorrow the sea of music will spread still further. Knowledge embodied in intricate machines will make accessible to anyone what in the past belonged only to a few. Music will come to our homes in all its grandeur of uncorrupted and enriched beauty. This is guaranteed by the continuous development of electroacoustics, sound recording, and radio.

Before long our music rooms and concert-halls will change out of all recognition. In the new buildings the listener will hear music equally well from any place. Not that we have to wait for this to happen. You will find ideal acoustics in quite a number of existing halls, such as the auditorium in the Kremlin's Palace of Congresses.

Electroacoustics will add more beauty to familiar sounds and will put over to the audience the most subtle nuances of music which are now imperceptible.

Singers will no longer have to strain their voices against the orchestra. High-fidelity sound-reinforcing equipment and electrical tone-quality control will promote a new vocal art, far more refined and profound than it is now.

Auditoriums will no longer have that unsightly orchestra pit. The orchestra will face the audience. Probably the conductor will also follow suit. Optics and television will show musical performance intimately associated with creative inspiration.

Scriabin's dream—a reunion of the arts, especially tone and colour, will come true. This composer strongly believed in building up music with flashes, blazes and glows. As Scriabin (and some of his predecessors) thought, the listener should not only be given something to hear but also something to see.

He wrote a line for 'a keyboard of light' in the score of his *Prometheus* and built a device to throw a play of colour on to a screen. It was very crude, lamps of different colours, wires and switches. It was the first attempt, and a very timid one.

After Scriabin a good many talented and purposeful engineers and musicians worked on his idea. A whole range of 'keyboards of light' have been made, including a harmonium in which every key turns on a lamp of a definite colour. Some of them, instead of lamps, use prisms which project on to a screen various hues and tints, blending and changing them continually.

More recently, a group of enthusiasts in Kazan (University and Conservatoire students) decoded Scriabin's part for 'a keyboard of light' in his *Prometheus,* built ingenious electronic instruments (called Prometheus-*I* and Prometheus-*II*) and played it as conceived by the composer. The performance was a great success. Some of the newspaper critics simply raved about it.

In another system, music itself produces its own accompaniment in light. This is done in an electroacoustical-optical converter built by the inventor Konstantin Leontyev and Professor A. Ya. Lerner of the Automation and Telecontrol Institute. The machine gives man a paradoxical power—'to hear with his eyes'. Based on an elegant hypothesis relating sight and hearing, the apparatus conveys sound information to the brain through the eyes. It listens to music with its microphone, analyzes it at once, prepares an appropriate play of colour, and produces it for the audience to see.

Leontyev's machine set off heated debates among musicians which are still going on. It has many opponents. To them its effects seem too deliberate. It also has staunch supporters, such as Kara-Karayev, a prominent Soviet composer.

The chances are that we shall live to see fantastic light effects accompany soloists, orchestras and choirs. The happy union of tone and colour will produce so far unknown aesthetic and emotional experiences.

Smells, too, may be used to fortify the symphony of tone and colour. Some experiments have already been carried out. In the Aromarama, for example, the spectators were sprinkled with aromatic liquids or powders in perfect timing with the scenes on the screen. In another, more ingenious system, known as subliminal advertising, the words 'smell of a rose', 'smell of smoke', 'smell of a pine-tree', and so on are printed on some of the frames of the film being shown. The words follow at a rate too rapid to be seen consciously. The spectator is sure of seeing the scenes of the film. But subconsciously 'smell information' has time to reach his brain and suggest an appropriate response. This device may well be used in music. But Leontyev's hypothesis will hardly work here; you can't possibly transmit 'sound information' through smell or 'listen with your nose'.

Use may also be made of a moving floor in the auditorium. Way back, in the 1930's Thérémin studied the effect of a rising and sinking floor during a musical performance. Sometimes, he found, the joint action of sound and motion gave the listeners an unforgettable experience— keen, entrancing, almost hypnotic. Thérémin obtained a similar effect in an auditorium with a stationary floor by raising and lowering a pattern projected onto a white wall at the rear. At the sight of a 'rising' wall the listeners' hearts sank. They felt as if they were falling down.

Thérémin went as far as to try and make the sense of touch serve music. He had strips of fabric built into the arm-rests of the chairs in an auditorium. As the music was played, the strips moved under the listeners' palms, presenting their surfaces, now smooth and now velvety as appropriate. Thus all man's senses can be used for the purposes of musical art.

Today we can hardly imagine how many new instruments will be added to the orchestra in the future. They will be capable of intricate changes in tone quality, immense chords, consonances encompassing the remotest intervals now beyond the reach of any performing artist, and melodies in the purest modes and scales. Notes will be formed exactly like the human voice—by blending pure tones. This will give them a human quality and vital power. Instrumental music will be able to speak, laugh and cry in the direct meaning of these words.

Music synthesizers will obey man and give the composer an unprecedented freedom of creation. They will compose music and play any improvisations. In fact, this can already be done on the ANS. In the future truly universal musical instruments will come possessing much greater versatility and precision.

The performing artist will have greater freedom, too. He will be able to control the new instruments with his eyes and thoughts rather than by his lips or hands, as the violinist, the trumpeter or the pianist does today.

Although this may sound incredible, determined inventors have exactly this objective. Thirty years ago Thérémin could control the tone quality of his Théréminvox with his eyes. When playing his instrument, he had in front of him a strip carrying lenses. Behind each lens was a photo-cell connected to a separate tone control. The system was set to operate only when an image of the edge of the iris was projected onto a photo-cell. By shifting his eyes from lens to lens, the performer could change the tone quality at will, making the instrument now sound resonant and mellow, and now sharp and ringing.

Thérémin controlled the loudness by his thought. He wore a ring on his finger which conducted his biopotentials to a power amplifier, and the reinforced signal controlled the volume of sound. As he thought of changing the loudness, the biopotential in the finger varied, and the volume control moved up or down.

True, Thérémin got no further than experiments with his unorthodox techniques. Nor could he, because radio engineering and automation were not so advanced as they are now. Today the situation is different; we already have arm prostheses controlled by biopotentials, and we are gaining deeper insight into the electrical activity of the human body. So, sooner or later musical instruments will come which are controllable, probably, even by the subconscious desire of the artist. Man will inject his will and thoughts into the responsive machine which will be an extension of his fingers and nerves. Isn't that fantastic? Instead of being a slave of the machine, man is becoming its almighty master.

Looking further ahead, we can see with our mind's eye machines which reproduce musical thoughts, that internal music which every person hears when his or her "very soul is singing". We can imagine thought-controlled computers composing all sorts of music.

Everything in the boundless world of sound will serve the immortal human genius, the life-giving will of the artist. The musician of the future will not abandon the violin or the piano. Instead he will augment their aesthetic power, penetrability and range. He will be both a physicist and a poet and will make a happy union of knowledge and inspiration.

# Index

## A.

Accordion, 26
Acoustic montage, 193
Aeolian harp, 10
AGUJARI, Lucrezia, 59
ALLIN, Norman, 58
*Al'ud*, 33
AMATI, Andrea, 38
AMATI, Nicola, 38
American organ, 26
ARETINUS, Guido, 43
ARISTOXENUS, 128
Attack, 162
Aurochs, horn, 18
Automatic piano, 213

## B.

BACH, 28, 51, 121, 131
Bagpipe, 10
Bassoon, 10, 16, 74
Beating reeds, 27
*Bebung*, 44
BEETHOVEN, 44
BERLINER, Emile, 167
BERLIOZ, 18
BOEHM, Theobald, 15
*Bombarde*, 16
Bow, 34, 35
Brass instruments, 23, 74
BUSONI, 140

## C.

Cabinet organ, 26
CAHILL, Thaddeus, 139-40
CHALIAPIN, 103, 134, 172
*Chalumeau*, 17
Chronaxy, 103
*Churinga*, 9
Clarinet, 16, 17, 27, 74
Clarion, 21
Clavichord, 44, 45-7,
 unfretted, 45
Comma of Didymus, 129
 of Pythagoras, 128, 129, 130
Concertina, 26
Consonance, 120
Contra bassoon, 16
Cornet, 23
CRISTOFORI, Bartolommeo, 49-53
CTESIBIUS, 26
Cup mouthpiece, 20

## D.

DENNER, Johann Christian, 17
*Domra*, 36
Double bassoon, 16
Double reed, 16
Double-string lyre, 29

*Doudka*, 8
Dulcimer, 43, 50
Dynamophone, 139-40

## E.

EDISON, 167
Egyptian harp, 30
Ekvodin, 158
Electrical instruments, principles of, 138-39
ELLINGTON, Duke, 207
Etherophone, 144

## F.

*Fagotto*, 16
FESPER, Caspar, 58
Fiddle, 34, 35-6
Fifth, wolf's, 129
Finger-board, 33
Finger-stopping, 33
Fingering, 28
Fipple, 12
Flageolet tone, 74
*Flauto dolce*, 12
Flute, 11, 16, 23
*Flute douce*, 12
Formants, 105-06
Four-stringed lute, 33
French horn, 21, 23, 74
Frets, 33

## G.

*Geige*, 36
German flute, 12
MAGGINI, Giovanni Paolo, 38
GUARNERI, Giuseppe, 38
GLAREAN, 122
*Goudok*, 8, 36
Gourd bow, 29

*Gousli*, 8, 36
Gramophone, 167
Grand piano, 7, 42, 126
*Gravicembalo col piano e forte*, 50
Greek lyre, 30
Guitar, 34, 36
*Gunbi*, 30, 32
Gut, 32

## H.

HAMMOND, Laurence, 151
Hamograph, 205
HANDEL, 28, 131
Harmonica, 26
Harmonics, aural, 114, 117
Harmonium, 26
Harmony, 119
Harp, 29-31, 46
Harpsichord, 45-7, 50
HAYDN, 44
Hearing, 111-13
HELMHOLTZ, 70-3, 111-19, 133
HILLER, 230
*Hu ch'in*, 8, 35
Hunting horn, 18
Hunting-horn band, 19
*Hydraulis*, 26
Illiac, 230
Infra-sound, 57-8
Intervals, musical, 127
 natural, 129, 133
 tempered, 133
ISAACSON, 230

## J.

Jacks, 45
Jaws' harp, 10
*Jongleur*, 35
JOSEPH DEL GESU, 38

## K.

Key note, 123
Keyboard instruments, vs. electrophonic, 156
*Kichara*, 30
*Kissar*, 29, 30, 31, 32
Krystadine, 159

## L.

LEIBNITZ, 114
LEONARDO DA VINCI, 47-8
Lip technique, 21
Lip-reed instrument, 18
LULLY, Jean Baptiste, 14
LUPOT, Nicolas, 42
Lute, 34, 46

## M.

MA SU-CHIEN, 228
Mandolin, 34
Manuals, 27
MARTENOT, 151
Mode, Ionian, 122
    Lydian, 122
    minor, 120, 121
Monochord, 43
Mouth organ, 24
Mouthpiece, 21
MOZART, 46, 53, 59
Music, computer, 225
    in U.S.S.R., 231-36
    perspectives, 236-38
Musical boxes, 212-13

## N.

NERNST, Walter, 152
*Niastarangha*, 9

## O.

Oboe, 16, 74
Octave, 126-27
    Pythagorean, 128
OLSON, 205
Ondes Musicales, 151
Organ, 23, 25-6, 27, 129, 133
    Hammond, 152
    transistor, 159
Organ beater, 28
Organ playing, 27-8
Overblowing, 20, 23

## P.

PAGANINI, 38
PALESTRINA, Giovanni da, 120
Pan's pipes, 28
Phonogene, 205
Phonograph, 167
Piano, 34, 44, 51-4, 129, 133
    Neo-Bechstein, 152
    upright, 53
Piano keys, 27
Piano player, 213
Piano-accordion, 26
Pianoforte, 50
*P'i p'a*, 8, 33
Pitch, standard concert, 58
Plectrum, 46
Polyphony, 43
*Pommern*, 16
Portable organ, 26
Psaltery, 43, 45
PYTHAGORAS, 127
Quills, 45
*Quite-de-loup*, 129

## R.

RAMEAU, Jean Philippe, 130
*Ravanstron*, 35
*Rebab*, 31, 35
Rebec, 36
Recorder flute, 12, 14
Reed pipe, 16
Resonance, 68, 73
Resonator, 60, 68-70, 73-4, 76

## S.

Sackbut, 22
*Sacqueboute*, 22
SAVART, Félix, 77-9
SAX, Adolphe (Antoine), 17
Saxophone, 17
Scale, chromatic, 122
   diatonic, 122
   just intonation, 128-29
      major, 120, 121, 122
      mean-tone temperament, 129
      minor, 120, 121
      pentatonic, 122
      Pythagorean, 127-29
      twelve-interval, equal-temperament, 130-31, 132
SCHAEFFER, Myron, 205
SCHAEFFER, Pierre, 205
SCRIABIN, 134-35
SEGOVIA, 152
Serpent, 10
Shawm, 17
*Sheng*, 24, 27
Shepherd's horn, 20
SHOLPO, 187-204
Side-blown flute, 12, 13
Signal horn, 20
SILBERMAN, Gottfried, 51
*Skomorokh*, 36
*Scrypitsa*, 36
Sonor, 153
Sound recording, magnetic means, 169
   on film, 168-69, 191-92
   processed voices, 181-82
   reverberations, 175-78
   special effects, 182-84
   superposition, 174-75
   taped actuality, 184-86
   updating, 171-74
Sound studio, 169-71
Sound synthesizer, 212, 214-20, 222-24
Sound-box, 31, 32
Soundboard, 46
   piano, 53
Sounds, musical, classification, 58-9
   def., 56-7
STAINER, Jacob, 42
STEIN, Johann, 53
Stereophonics, 179-80
STRADIVARIUS, Antonius, 37-42
String, as vibrator, 61, 66-8
Strings, 32
   metal, 46
   unison, 46
Symphony orchestra, 7, 28, 157
Synthetic music, hand-drawn, 187-89
*Syrinx*, 24

## T.

Tangents, 43, 44, 45
TARTINI, Giuseppe, 113
Telharmonium, 139-40

*Terzi souni*, 113
THEREMIN, 141-51
Théréminvox, 144-51
Third, major, 120
    minor, 120
Tonality, 123
Tone colour, electrophonic, 161-62
Tones, classification, 65, 73-4
    combination, 113
    difference, 114, 115
    fundamental, 119
    ratio of frequencies, 120
    summation, 119
Tonic, 123
Transverse flute, 12
Trautonium, 151
TRAUTWEIN, 151
Trembita, 18
Tremor, 44
Trombone, 22
Trummscheidt, 10
Trumpet, 74
Trumpet marine, 10
Tuba, 23
Tuning, 123, 124
    Pythagorean, 128
Tuning pegs, 30

## V.

Valve, 22-5
Valve trumpet, 23

Variophone, 194
*Vibrato*, 100-01
Vibrator, 60-1, 63, 69
*Vina*, 33
Violin, 7, 34, 36-42, 76, 77
    scientific manufacture, 80-1
    Soviet research, 81-8, 91-7
    vs. electrophonics, 144
VITRUVIUS, 56
Voice analysis, 98-110
VULLAUME, Jean-Baptiste, 78

## W.

*Waldhorn*, 21
*Wambee*, 30, 32
WERCKMEISTER, 130, 132
Whizzer, 9
Woodwinds, 17, 74

## Y.

YOUNG, Thomas, 61-8, 72
Young's laws, 65-8

## Z.

*Zourna*, 16, 36
ZARLINO, 128

## TO THE READER

Mir Publishers would be glad to have your opinion on the translation and the design of this book.

Please send all suggestions to Mir Publishers, 2, Pervy Rizhsky Pereulok, Moscow, USSR.

*Printed in the Union of Soviet Socialist Republics*